D0209928

THE SEARCH FOR SIGNS OF

INTELLIGENT LIFE

IN THE UNIVERSE

THE SEARCH FOR SIGNS OF

INTELLIGENT LIFE

IN THE UNIVERSE

BY JANE WAGNER

Perennial

An Imprint of HarperCollins*Publishers*

ACKNOWLEDGMENTS

For all their help and support, many thanks to Craig Nelson, Pat Kingsley, Sam Cohn, Arlene Donovan, Charles Bowden, Paula Laurence, Leo Lerman, Annie Leibovitz, Lydia Link and Lily Tomlin.

Thanks also to the staff and crew of the play which premiered September 26, 1985, at the Plymouth Theater in New York City: Veronica Claypool, Otts Munderloh, Cheryl Dolby, Catherine Olim, Cheryl Swannack, Pamela Young, Bruce Cameron, Phyllis Della, Kirk Bookman, Kurt Fischer, Madelaine Wing, Judy Van Herpen, Richard Tomlin, Tina-Marie Marquis, Luanne Withee

and

| Neil Peter Jampolis | Ann Roth | Janet Beroza |
| scenery and lighting | costumes | production stage manager |

Photo Credits: Page 240

THE SEARCH FOR SIGNS OF INTELLIGENT LIFE IN THE UNIVERSE. Copyright © 1986, 1990 by Jane Wagner Inc. Afterword © 1985 by Belles-Lettres, Inc. All rights reserved. Printed in the United States of America. No part of this book may be used or reproduced in any manner whatsoever without written permission except in the case of brief quotations embodied in critical articles and reviews. For information address HarperCollins Publishers Inc., 10 East 53rd Street, New York, NY 10022.

HarperCollins books may be purchased for educational, business, or sales promotional use. For information please write: Special Markets Department, HarperCollins Publishers Inc., 10 East 53rd Street, New York, NY 10022.

Designer: Barbara Richer
Collages: Jane Wagner
Contributing Photographers: Annie Leibovitz, Martha Swope, Vladimir Bliokh, f. Stop Fitzgerald
Graphics Production: Jerri Allyn, Clsuf, Fraver, Rubin Raimundi, Chris Scheller, Cheryl Swannack, Luanne Withee
A Tomlin and Wagner Theatricalz Production

First Perennial Library edition published 1987. First HarperPerennial edition published 1990. Reprinted in Perennial 2000.

Library of Congress Cataloging-in-Publication Data

Wagner, Jane.
The search for signs of intelligent life in the universe.

"Perennial Library"

Based on: the Broadway play written by Wagner starring Lily Tomlin.
I. Title.
PS3573.A3863S4   1987   8122'.54   86-45435
ISBN 0-06-092071-8(pbk.)

00 01 02 03 04   RRD(H) 20 19 18 17 16 15 14 13 12 11

PART I

Here we are, standing on the corner of
"Walk, Don't Walk."
You look away from me, tryin' not to catch my eye,
but you didn't turn fast enough, *did* you?

You don't like my *raspy* voice, do you?
I got this *raspy* voice
'cause I have to yell all the time
'cause nobody around here ever
LISTENS to me.

You don't like that I scratch so much; yes, and excuse me,
I scratch so much
'cause my neurons are
on *fire*.

And I admit my smile is not at its Pepsodent best
'cause I think my
caps must've somehow got
osteo*porosis.*

And if my eyes seem to be twirling around like fruit flies—
the better to see you with, my dears!

Look at me,
you mammalian-brained LUNKHEADS!
I'm not just talking to myself. I'm talking to you, too.
And to you
and you
and you
and you and you and you!

I know what you're thinkin'; you're thinkin' I'm crazy.
You think I give a hoot? You people
look at my shopping bags,
call me crazy 'cause I save this junk. What should we call the
ones who
buy it?

It's my belief we all, at one time or another,
secretly ask ourselves the question,
"Am *I* crazy?"
In my case, the answer came back: A resounding
YES!

You're thinkin': How does a person know if they're crazy
or not? Well, sometimes you don't know. Sometimes you
can go through life suspecting you *are*
but never really knowing for sure. Sometimes you know for sure
'cause you got so many people tellin' you you're crazy
that it's your word against everyone else's.

Another sign is when you see life so clear sometimes
you black out.
This is your typical visionary variety
who has flashes of insight
but can't get anyone to listen to 'em
'cause their insights make 'em sound so *crazy!*

In my case,
the symptoms are subtle
but unmistakable to the trained eye. For instance,
here I am,
standing at the corner of "Walk, Don't Walk,"
waiting for these aliens from outer space to show up.
I call that crazy, don't you? If I were sane,
I should be waiting for the light like everybody else.

They're late
as usual.

You'd think,
as much as they know about time travel,
they could be on time *once* in a while.

I could kick myself.
I told 'em I'd meet 'em on the corner of "Walk, Don't Walk"
'round lunchtime.
Do they even know what "lunch" means?
I doubt it.

And " 'round." Why did I say " 'round"? Why wasn't I more
specific? This is so typical of what I do.

Now they're probably stuck somewhere in time, wondering
what I meant by
" 'round lunchtime." And when they get here, they'll be
dying to know what "lunchtime" means. And when they
find out it means going to Howard Johnson's for fried
clams, I wonder, will they be just a bit let down?

I dread having to explain
tartar sauce.

This problem of time just points out
how far apart we really are.
See, our ideas about time and space are different
from theirs. When we think of time, we tend to think of
clock radios, coffee breaks, afternoon naps, leisure time,
halftime activities, parole time, doing time, Minute Rice, instant
tea, mid-life crises, that time of the month, cocktail hour.
And if I should suddenly
mention *space*—aha! I bet most of you thought of your
closets. But when they think of time and space, they really think
of
Time and Space.

They asked me once my thoughts on infinity and I told 'em
with all I had to think about, infinity was not on my list
of things to think about. It could be time on an ego trip,
for all I know. After all, when you're pressed for time,
infinity may as well
not be there.
They said, to them, infinity is
time-released time.

Frankly, infinity doesn't affect
me personally one way or the other.

You think too long about infinity, you could go
stark raving mad.
But I don't ever want to sound negative about going crazy.
I don't want to overromanticize it either, but frankly,
goin' crazy was the *best* thing ever happened to me.
I don't say it's for everybody;
some people couldn't cope.

But for me it came at a time when nothing else seemed to be
working. I got the kind of madness Socrates talked about,
"A divine release of the soul from the yoke of
custom and convention." I refuse to be intimidated by
reality anymore.
After all, what is reality anyway? Nothin' but a
collective hunch. My space chums think reality was once a
primitive method of
crowd control that got out of hand.
In my view, it's absurdity dressed up
in a three-piece business suit.

I made some studies, and
reality is the leading cause of stress amongst those in
touch with it. I can take it in small doses, but as a lifestyle
I found it too confining.
It was just too needful;
it expected me to be there for it *all* the time, and with all
I have to do—
I had to let something go.

Now, since I put reality on a back burner, my days are
jam-packed and fun-filled. Like some days, I go hang out
around Seventh Avenue; I love to do this old joke:
I wait for some music-loving tourist from one of the hotels
on Central Park to go up and ask someone,
"How do I get to Carnegie Hall?"
Then I run up and yell,
"Practice!"
The expression on people's faces is priceless. I never
could've done stuff like that when I was in my *right* mind.
I'd be worried people would think I was *crazy.*
When I think of the fun I missed,
I try not to be bitter.

See, the human mind is kind of like . . .

a piñata. When it breaks open,
there's a lot of surprises inside. Once you get the piñata
perspective, you see that losing your mind
can be a peak experience.

I was not always a bag lady, you know.
I used to be a designer and creative consultant. For big
companies!
Who do you think thought up the color scheme
for Howard Johnson's?
At the time, nobody was using
orange and aqua
in the same room together.
With fried clams.

Laugh tracks:
I gave TV sitcoms the idea for canned laughter.
I got the idea, one day I heard voices
and no one was there.

Who do you think had the idea to package panty hose
in a plastic goose egg?

One thing I personally don't like about panty hose:
When you roll 'em down to the ankles the way I like 'em, you
can't walk too good. People seem amused, so what's a little
loss of dignity? You got to admit:
It's a look!

The only idea I'm proud of—

my umbrella hat. Protects against sunstroke, rain and
muggers. For *some* reason, muggers steer clear of people
wearing umbrella hats.

So it should come as no shock . . . I am now creative consultant to
these aliens from outer space. They're a kinda cosmic
fact-finding committee. Amongst other projects, they've been
searching all over for Signs of Intelligent Life.

It's a lot trickier than it sounds.

We're collecting all kinds of data
about life here on Earth. We're determined to figure out,
once and for all, just what the hell it all means.
I write the data on these Post-its and then we study it.
Don't worry, before I took the consulting job, I gave 'em my whole
psychohistory.

I told 'em what drove *me* crazy was my *last* creative consultant
job, with the Ritz Cracker mogul, Mr. Nabisco. It was
my job to come up with snack inspirations to increase sales.
I got this idea to give Cracker Consciousness to the entire
planet.

I said, "Mr. Nabisco, sir! You could be the first to sell the concept of munching to the Third World. We got an untapped market here! These countries got millions and millions of people don't even know where their next *meal* is *coming* from. So the idea of eatin' *between* meals is somethin' just never occurred to 'em!"

I heard myself sayin' *this!*

Must've been when I went off the deep end.
I woke up in the nuthouse. They were hookin' me up.
One thing they don't tell you about shock treatments, for months afterwards you got
flyaway hair. And it used to *be* my best feature.

See, those shock treatments gave me new electrical circuitry (frankly, I think one of the doctors' hands must've been wet). I started having these time-space continuum shifts, I guess you'd call it. Suddenly, it was like my central nervous system had a patio addition out back.
Not only do I have a linkup to extraterrestrial channels. I also got a hookup with humanity as a whole. Animals and plants, too. I used to talk to plants all the time; then, one day, they started talking back. They said,
"Trudy,
shut up!"

I got like this . . .

built-in Betamax in my head. Records anything.
It's like somebody's using my brain to dial-switch
through humanity. I pick up signals that seem to transmit
snatches of people's lives.
My umbrella hat works as a satellite dish. I hear this
sizzling sound like white noise. Then I know it's
trance time.
That's how I met my space chums. I was in one of my trances,
watching a scene from someone's life, and I suddenly sense
others were there
watching with me.

Uh-oh.
I see this skinny
punk kid.
Got hair the color of
Froot Loops and she's wearin' a T-shirt says "Leave Me Alone."
There's a terrible family squabble going on.
If they're listening to each other,
they're all gonna get their feelings hurt.

I see glitches—
Now I see this dark-haired actress
on a Broadway stage. I know her. I see her all the time outside
the Plymouth Theater, Forty-fifth Street.

L
I
L
Y

I'm so glad that you came tonight.
I sometimes worry no one will show up, and without you,
there'd be little point
in me being here.

I think you should know I worry a lot.
Like the Nobel sperm bank. Something bothers me about the
world's greatest geniuses
sitting around
reading pornography
and jerking off.

I worry that humanity has been "advanced" to its present level
of incompetency
because evolution works on
the Peter Principle.

I worry that Andy Warhol may be right—

And everyone *will* be famous for fifteen minutes.
How will there ever be room for us all
at Betty Ford's?

I even worry about reflective flea collars. Oh, sure, drivers can
see them glow in the dark
but so can the fleas.

I worry if peanut oil comes from peanuts
and olive oil comes from olives, where *does*
baby oil come from?

One thing I have no worry about is whether
God exists.
But it has occurred to me that God has Alzheimer's and has
forgotten
we exist.

I worry that our lives are like
soap operas. We can go for months and not
tune in to them, then six months later

we look in and the
same stuff
is still going on.

I worry whoever thought up the term "quality control"
thought if we didn't control it,
it would get out of hand.

I worry no matter how cynical you become,
it's never enough to keep up.

I worry where tonight fits in the Cosmic Scheme of things.
I worry there *is* no Cosmic Scheme to things.

T
R
U
D
Y
Dial-switch me outta this!
I got enough worries of my own.
These trances are entertaining but distracting, especially since
someone *else* has the remote control, and if the pause button
should somehow get punched, I could have a neurotransmitter
mental meltdown. Causes "lapses of the synapses." I forget
things. Never underestimate the power of the human mind to
forget. The other day, I forgot where I put my house keys—
looked everywhere, then I remembered
I don't have a house. I forget more important things, too.
Like the meaning of life.
I forget that.
It'll come to me, though.
Let's just hope when it does,
I'll be in. . . .

My space chums say they're learning so much about us
since they've begun to time-share my trances.
They said to me, "Trudy, the human mind is so-o-o strange."
I told 'em, "That's nothin' compared to the human genitals."

Next to my trances they love goin' through my shopping bags.
Once they found this old box of Cream of Wheat. I told 'em, "A
box of cereal." But they saw it as a picture of infinity. You know
how on the front is a picture of that guy holding up a box of
Cream of Wheat
and on *that* box is a picture of that guy holding up a box of
Cream of Wheat
and on *that* box is a picture of that guy holding up a box of
Cream of Wheat
and on *that* box is a picture of that guy holding up a box of
Cream of Wheat . . .

We think so different.

They find it hard to grasp some things that come easy to us,
because they simply don't have our frame of reference.
I show 'em this can of Campbell's tomato soup.
I say,
"This is soup."
Then I show 'em a picture of Andy Warhol's painting
of a can of Campbell's tomato soup.
I say,
"This is art."

"This is soup."

"And this is art."

Then I shuffle the two behind my back.

Now what is this?

No,
this is soup
and *this is art*!

Oh, there's that sound!
Here we go again. Looks like we're
somewhere . . . in suburbia. A housewife. Hey,
I've seen this woman before. She used to sell
Tupperware.

JUDITH BEASLEY

About a month ago, I was shown some products designed to
improve the sex lives of suburban housewives. I got so
excited,
I just had to come on public access and tell you about it. To
look at *me,* you'd *never suspect* I was a semi-nonorgasmic
woman. This means it was *possible* for me to have an orgasm—
but highly unlikely.

To me, the term "sexual freedom" meant freedom from having to
have sex. And then along came Good Vibrations. And was I
surprised! Now I am a regular
Cat on a Hot Tin Roof.

As a love object,
it surpasses my husband Harold by a country mile.
But please,
this is no threat to the family unit;
think of it as a kind of
Hamburger Helper for the boudoir.

Can you afford one, you say?
Can you afford *not* to have one, I say.
Why, the *time* it saves alone is worth the price.
I'd rank it up there with Minute Rice,
Reddi-Wip
and Pop-Tarts.

Ladies, it simply takes the guesswork out of making love.

"But doesn't it kill romance?" you say.
And I say,
"What doesn't?"

So what'll it be? This deluxe kit? Or this purse-size model
for the "woman on the go"? Fits anywhere and comes with a
silencer to avoid
curious onlookers.

Ladies, it can be a real help to the busy married woman who has
a thousand chores and simply does not need the extra burden of
trying to have an
orgasm.

But what about guilt, you say? Well, that thought did cross
my mind.

But at one time I felt guilty using a cake mix instead of
baking from scratch.

I learned to live with that.
I can learn to live with this.

T
R
U
D
Y

I hear ... music ...
I see this young woman
at her aerobics class. She's the only one working out
in dangling earrings
and clanking bracelets.

Whooo!

Shake it out!

I've been on four job interviews today, Eileen; I've got one more
to go.
I lost my job with the answering service because I would not
lie for people who wanted me to say they were out
when they weren't. These days,
integrity is not a required skill.

This may sound like a cop-out, but some of my job probs are not
my fault. I'm dyslexic, they tell me.

I don't type, file or spell well. It's hard to type when you
can't spell
and it's hard to file when everything you've typed looks like
alphabet soup.

I'd do better at something creative, and I feel I *am* somewhat
creative, but some*how* I *lack* talent to go with it, and *being*
creative without talent is a bit like being a perfectionist
and not being able to do anything right.

All my life I've always wanted to *be* somebody.
But I see now I should have been more
specific.

It's not that I lack ambition. I *am* ambitious in the sense that I
want to be more than I am now. But if I were truly
ambitious, I think I'd already *be* more than I am now.

A sobering thought, Eileen:
What if, right at this very moment,
I *am* living up to my full potential?

I've about reached the conclusion if I'm ever going to make
something of my life, chances are it won't be through work.
It will have to be through personal growth stuff.

Go for the burn!

I've been trying to get into positive thinking in a really big way.
Frankly, I think it's my only hope.

My seminar leader said to me, "Chrissy, you should learn
to be happy
one day at a time." But what I learned from that is that you can
also be *miserable*
one day at a time.

This seminar I'm in, Eileen, has opened me up like some kind of
bronchial *spray*. I got clear:
my expectations about life are simply way too high. So are yours,
I bet, Eileen, because we
are all being *force-fed* a lot of false hopes about romance,
success, sex, life—you name it.

My seminar leader said to me, "Chrissy, you are a classic
'false hope' case" . . . because not only do I not have a very firm
grasp on reality, see,
but I have sort of a loose grip on my fantasies, too.

We had this exercise, Eileen.
We played this mind game called
"We know everything we need to know
if only we knew it."
We were told to be silent and our minds would tell
us whatever we needed to know.

I flashed on the time I lost my contact lens. There I was
looking for my contact lens
which I couldn't find
because I had lost my contact lens.
I thought: Wow, the story of my *life*.

You can't expect insights, even the big ones,
to suddenly make you understand
everything. But I figure: Hey, it's a step if they leave you
confused
in a deeper way.

The seminar ends tonight. To get us to face our fears,
we're supposed to walk over this bed of really red-hot coals—
barefoot. Quite a test! You name
it; I've feared it.
Except walking over hot coals . . . I never had that fear
till just now.

I'm working on overcoming my fears, Eileen,
but it's not easy.
At the Phobia Institute once,
this guy in group told about a friend who was terrified
of driving on the freeway,
but finally she conquered her fear and got so she thought
nothing of driving on the freeway.
And guess what?
She died
in a freeway accident.
That story has always stuck with me.

But *my* fears are more subtle. Like I fear being out of work,
and yet when I'm working, I have this constant fear
of being fired. The worst fear I have
is that this feeling I once had may come back.

At the lockers

Once . . . I've been wanting to tell someone this, Eileen . . .
once I came *this* close
to committing suicide.
That's how down and low I felt.
I would have, too. There was just one thing stopped me.
Fear. I was just plain too afraid.
So, if I ever did commit suicide, I'd have to be so desperate
I wouldn't even let fear of suicide
stand in my way.

And yet if I could overcome a fear like that
I could overcome
all my fears, I bet.

And then, of course—
and here's the irony—probably
if I weren't afraid, I'd really want to live.
Only, by then, if I'd really conquered my fear of suicide,
it might be too late.
I might already, you know,
have done it.

Life can be so ironic. Sometimes, to make any move at all seems
totally pointless. I bet the worst part about dying is the part where
your whole life passes before you.

I hope I don't ever feel that low again. At the moment, I feel
pretty up about the work I'm doing on myself. I used to be so
sensitive; sometimes I would think of the Kennedy family and I
would just burst out in tears. I'm not so sensitive anymore; I
don't burst out in tears as much as I used to and I hardly ever
think of the Kennedys anymore. So these seminars have been
good for me, Eileen, which is more than I can say for any job I've
ever had.

Course, *I* don't want to be a seminar-*hopper,* like this
ex-friend I used to know. She had no time for *any*thing but

self-improvement. She felt she had outgrown everyone,
especially *me*. Behind my back, she told this person that *I* was an
Upwardly
Immobile Asshole. And then, to add insult to injury,
she said it to my face. That did it—
I get enough insults on job interviews.

Well, I guess I'll see you tomorrow. How they lied about
this health club! Talk about false hopes. "The *place* to get
thin and meet good-looking men." The good-looking men here
are mostly looking at themselves.

I have never gotten so much as a date for cappuccino.

Yet I keep coming. I'm keeping really fit, I tell myself.
But the truth is,
I pig out one week and starve the next.

I have gained and lost
the same ten pounds
so many times over and over again
my cellulite must have déjà vu.

And all that business about exercise releasing endorphins.
I have not felt so much as *one* endorphin being released. Once
more, false hopes.

But hey, if it weren't for false hopes, the economy would
just collapse, I bet. Oh. I better hurry. My job interview! This
time I could get lucky. Requires no skills;
I'll just be hooking people up to
bio-feedback machines. At least I won't be lying to them.
Well, slinkydinks, I'm outta here.

P A U L

This body-building bit, Ted: lately I've been thinking
what's the point a lot.
Like what's the point being a health nut by day if you're a coke
head at night. What worries me, I'm getting burned out
on both. I used to get a charge knowing my body was so great
I could turn heads. Now, when I sense some girl digging me,
I don't get so turned on; instead, I get this
trapped feeling.

The thought occurs, Ted: What if I run out
of things to get off on?

Even sports. Sure, I still watch the
games, but I don't root so much anymore,
just watch. Hell, it was the rooting that made it worthwhile.

It's the same with sex!
Yeah, my sex urge is still industrial strength,
but where's the desire?
I miss the disco scene, man.
I feel about the disco days what
hippies must feel about Woodstock.

I blame a lot of what I'm going through on Penny—
the divorce thing sure threw me for a loop.
Took the wind outta my sails. You mind if I talk, Ted?
You got time? I still can't get over it: Penny and I, we had
a romance like something Lionel Richie might sing
about. Then it just all started to fall
apart. One day, I'm in the den, waiting for the
game to start, I see this magazine quiz
Penny's been filling out: "On a Scale
of One to Ten, How Do You Rate Your Man?"
As a dresser, a dancer, a conversationalist, a lover? She'd
given me a three on everything. A three!
After that, making love with her
was never the same. A three!

Hell, who knows what's considered a good
lover these days anyway? Every time you turn around
there's a new erogenous zone you gotta go explore:
clitoris, vaginal, X marks the G spot, the back
of the knee. Hell, these days, a guy needs his
cock hooked up to an Apple computer.

Okay, all right, I was no angel.
One night—Penny was pregnant; she wasn't
feeling well. We'd just moved;
there was a lot of tension. So I pop into this disco to decompress.
I see this hot-looking chick, Marge. I'd seen her there before—
a real knockout. So we do some coke—seemed innocent
enough at the time—she keeps coming on to me.
In a moment of weakness, I go with her to her pad over her plant
store. We smoke some wacko weed she grew herself. This is the
kind of woman . . .
I wake up with the imprint of her Mark Cross rape whistle
on my chest.

She starts asking me all kinds of questions
about my family background—my talents, my IQ. She loves it
that I have these eyes like David Bowie. See, look, Ted,
one green and one blue? You never noticed? Turns out she wants
me to be a sperm donor to these two friends of hers who want a
baby. So, I'm in a weird mood, I say, "Hell, why not?"
Then she gives me this turkey baster, wants me to
ejaculate into it. I freaked at first, but then she explained it
and it made perfect sense. So I did it. The drugs and all.
I got caught up in the moment.
Then, of course, when I came down, I think of
Penny . . . pregnant and all . . . the guilt hits me
like a karate chop. So I go home and tell Penny
everything that happened
'cause we'd made this promise that we wouldn't let lies start
building up between us.
That was my real mistake—telling her. I was so sure she'd
forgive me and we'd be back on track. Well, I was wrong;

I should've just let the lies pile up. The one time in my life I
make a conscious effort to be honest
and it blows up in my face.

Few weeks later, Penny has the baby. Can I
show you something? See this? Polaroid. Nurse
took it at the moment of my son's birth.
That's me and Penny in the delivery
room, breathing like two hippos with
a chest cold. I was right there. Penny wanted
the bonding thing that's
supposed to happen. You know what?
The bonding thing did happen, but then,
a few years later, so did the divorce. That's Paul
Junior—see, there's his little head peeping out. Isn't
life too much? Now I can see the beauty!
But at the time I almost passed out.

Penny's remarried, moved to Georgia;
I haven't seen little Paulie since . . . too long. Lately I been
thinking of that Marge chick and her friends—
the thought occurs, Ted, that maybe I've got this secret kid.
Chances are I have, 'cause I probably got a sperm count
like the national deficit.

There was one time on TV I see this genius—child prodigy or
something—playing the violin
like he was possessed. I almost switch channels, when it
suddenly hits me like a karate chop—
the kid looks like me when I was *his* age. I just about freak. I try
to get a close look at his eyes.
I could swear one was blue and one was green. I even go call
the station,
but they said they weren't allowed to take messages like that. So
anyway the girl I'm with tells me
I'm nutto and shows me how much coke I'd done. So I guess I let
my imagination run away with me,
but I still think, you know, "What if?"

Once, I obsessed to the point I go back to
the plant store thinking maybe I could talk Marge into
telling me, do I have this secret kid or not? All they
tell me at the store is Marge is dead. Blew me away.
She'd practically be
the godmother of my kid.

But I get these psychic flashes sometimes; I feel almost sure,
except for the genius part,
that could've been my kid.
I am very psychic, Ted.
Like sometimes, I can tune in to a rerun of *Twilight Zone* and I
somehow will sense before it begins
which episode it's going to be.

I can't stop thinking about it.
I ask myself, "What's he like?"
"Is he happy?" "Does he have the proper male role model?"
"Did the bonding thing happen,
I wonder?"

TRUDY

You've all had the
experience like somebody's on your wavelength . . .
well, think of how *I* must feel. . . . An elegant woman.
Rich type. Fendi bag, looks like. Jewelry.
Beautiful hands, too. Except the little finger on the
left hand has no tip.
Sits impatient . . . some beauty salon . . . could be the one
in Tramp's Tower. . . .

K
A
T
E

How much longer *must* I wait? I have read *all* the magazines.

I will *have* to be shampooed again.

Lonnie? Lonnie!
It's Kate.
No, I wasn't sure that that was *you,* either.

That's what comes of letting Bucci "the Arrogant" do our hair,
I suppose. I am here hoping Anouk
can do something to undo the
harm he's done. I mean, what is this?

This side ends
well above the left ear,
and this side ends,
as you can see, at the collarbone.

I am *sick* of being the victim
of trends I reflect
but don't even understand.

I tell *you,* coming here today was so humiliating. There were
people in the streets actually *staring* at my haircut.
People who normally would be *intimidated.*

Oh, I said to him, *"Please,* Bucci, nothing too radical." But
by *that* time, this side was *already* too radical. That's why
this side
looks *less* radical. Oh, well, I have gotten *scads* of
compliments. Especially when they see just *this* side
and not *this* side.

I have been waiting here so *long* today that soon this side
will *look* like this side.

Since I've been sitting here, two new age spots have appeared.
I hope they heard that.
Oh, well, I *do* like what it does for my cheekbones.
Well, *one* of my cheekbones. But you see, my left ear *juts*

out just where the cut is most radical. I'd like to say to him, "As
long as you *insist* on calling yourself an *artist,*
then go to Palm Beach and do oil portraits."
Well, no, no, I have never actually talked to him that way; can
you imagine what I would look like
if I ever actually talked to him that way?

Lonnie, you must read this article I've just finished.
Fascinating. It's all about how you can actually die
from boredom. Yes, "a slow, agonizing death."
They've done studies.

Have you ever used the expression "I am dying of boredom"?
Well, so have I; I have used it *all* my life. It says here if you
use it that often, that may be *exactly* what you are doing.

Even as I was *reading* this very *article,* in the back of my mind
I suddenly caught myself thinking:
How *boring!*

Guess who was at Rafael's last night?
With someone who was *not* her husband?
No, no, I will not *tell* you.
I will only say that she is someone you know. Rather well.
Now can you guess?

Her left ear *juts* out!
Yes, I am having an affair. But not for long,
I think. It's one thing to tolerate a boring marriage,
but a boring affair does *not* make sense.

I guess I'm talking about it because I think I *want* Freddie to
hear about it and get upset. Of course it has occurred to me
he might hear about it and *not* get upset.

Last year, I lost the tip off my little finger . . .

in a dreadful Cuisinart accident.
To this day, he has yet to notice.

And this haircut, Lonnie, hard to miss *this* haircut. Not a
word. I look at my disfigured fingertip. I think
how terrible that this should have happened
and yet it could have been worse. I have always loved music.
As a little girl I dreamed of being a concert violinist.
What a tragedy if my dream
had come true.

I'm going to L.A. next weekend to see a plastic surgeon
about a new fingertip. Maybe I should get him to operate
on this haircut while he is at it.
I can't stand the thought of going to L.A.
If you think I'm bored here,
you should see me there.

And I've got to go to the theater tonight, this actress/comedy
thing. They say it's
uplifting, but still I dread it. The last time they said
something was uplifting I must have dozed off during the
uplifting part. I don't know, Lonnie, am I so jaded
I can't be uplifted anymore,

or do I find being uplifted ultimately boring?
That is *really* jaded.
I don't know why I bother going; I can see it now—
I'll be just one big yawn
with a bad haircut.

Give me that magazine. Don't put it back.
I want to rip out that article
on boredom.

I'm going to have it Xeroxed and give copies to all my friends.
Now I know what's wrong with us all.
It says here—did you read?—"Having *everything* can
sometimes make you stop wanting *anything*."

It's called
"Rich People's Burn-Out."

And if *Town & Country* is writing about it,
a magazine not known for its psychological insight, well,
it must be of *epidemic* proportions, don't you think?

TRUDY

Uh-oh, irregular brain waves . . . another trance coming on.
I see that young woman again—the one with job probs.
She looks up from the classifieds.
I see tears in her eyes.
Now she takes up the newspapers . . .
throws them into the trash can. I don't like the look on her face.
She begins writing something . . .
a letter, looks like . . . now she stops, scratches something out.
Now she takes the dictionary, starts to look up a word,
now she's frantically thumbing through, having trouble trying to
find the word she wants.

New channel!
It's the skinny punk Froot Loop kid again.
Seems upset.

A A
G N
N G
U S
S T

Hello, Charlotte, listen, it is *vital* I stay
over at your house tonight!
Don't ask me to explain.
You've got to make your mom let me stay over!
Can't you force her to say yes?

Look, my parents think you're a bad influence on *me,*
too.

Just for that, you can't run the equipment at my gig tonight.

You are out of my life, Charlotte;

you are *her*story. You are the "crumb de la crumb." Drop off my
tapes at the Un-Club, or I'll sue you for all you're worth.
It is vital, Charlotte!

Don't you eyeball me, you *speck!* Can't you see I am USING this
PHONE!! And don't you *touch* that cage.
That's my parakeet in there.

Hello?
Look, it's vital I talk to the radio shrink. My name's Agnus.
I'm fifteen. My *parents* locked me out of the house today.
I want to find out if that is *legal.* I'm in the
ladies' room, House of Pancakes. I can't wait long.

Hello? Is this Dr. Kassorla, the psychologist? Look, Doctor,
for years I've been going home after school, nobody
would be there—

I'd take my key
from around my neck and
let myself in.
But today I go home,
I put my key in the door . . .

THEY CHANGED THE LOCKS ON ME!

Yeah, maybe it *was* something I did. I didn't say I was innocent.

Whatever I do is wrong, anyway. Like, last night, my stepmom,
she accuses me of leaving dirty fingerprints on the *cheese.*
Even getting an innocent piece of cheese becomes a criminal act.
But the problem goes deeper: My real mother's not around
much right now. She's in Europe, Germany or someplace,
doing her art thing. She's a performance artist. Like me.
There was this big custody beef, see, 'cause
my real mother's a lesbian. So the *court* gave me to my dad.
He's a gene-splicer, a bio-businessman at this research lab of
*mis*applied science. Where he's working on some new bio-form
he thinks he'll be able to patent.
He doesn't get that *I* am a new bio-form.

I AM USING THIS PHONE!! You IHOP speck!

So today I go by my dad's lab, to get some money for some gear
for my act,
and I see this like glob of bio-plasm
quivering there in this petri dish.
I don't know why I did it.
Maybe it was sibling rivalry.
But I leaned over
and I spit into it.
And of course, my dad had a MAD SCIENTIST ALERT! He says I've
ruined years of research.
The truth is he loves that *bio-form* more than *me.*

Yeah, I thought of calling the hot line for runaways, but I'm
worried maybe they don't take
throwaways like me. I have other family, my grandparents,
but we have nothing in common, except that we are all
carbon-based life forms.

What?
A commercial?
I can't believe you're brushing me off.
To sell some product
that probably killed some poor *lab rat.*
You've been about as helpful as an acid FLASHBACK!

TRUDY

She hangs up. Now she's walking out. She stops. She's thinking.
Now she takes the latchkey from around her neck
and throws it in the trash can.

AGNUS ANGST

Hey, where's my parakeet! Conway Tweety!

THAT CREEP! STOLE MY PARAKEET! Hey, you IHOP specks, you *must*
have seen somebody leave
with a cage. You all saw me come in with one. Don't you stare
at me with those *blueberry syrup mustaches!*

T R U D Y

In suburbia. An older couple sits watching TV. They're watching that woman who used to sell Tupperware.

L U D

Talkin' about vibrators that way!
The things you see on TV these days.
What kind of crazy world do we live in?

M A R I E

Lud, who was it said . . . ? that quote about, oh, you know . . .
What was that quote?
Do you remember, Lud?

L U D

Did you just hear what you said, Marie?

M A R I E

I reckon so. I just said it. . . .
What?

LUD   You were about to say somethin' *some*body said—you couldn't
think who said it or what it was they said.

MARIE   And that never happens to you, I suppose.
That never happens to him, does it, Fluffy?

LUD   Well, if I couldn't think who it was said somethin',
or what it was they said, I simply would not bring up the subject,
Marie. I'd simply keep my mouth shut.
Somethin' I wish *you'd* consider more often.

MARIE   I *used* to *tolerate* that kind of talk, because I told myself it was
your hernia made you act so *hateful.*
I have let you walk all over me.
Janet used to beg me, she'd say, "*Mama,* please join a
consciousness-raising group." I'd say, "Honey, what on earth
would I do at a consciousness-raising group?"

I missed out on it like I did everything else.

LUD   You know what your problem is, Marie?

MARIE   Yes. You!

LUD

You can't concentrate.

You've got a brain like a hummingbird. . . .

Makes you appear dense and at the same time flighty. Did you ever see a hummingbird try to make up its mind which flower to land on? Well, picture your brain
in place of that *bird*
and you have a clue as to what I have to put up with.

Some people have hare brains, some people have pea brains. And some people . . .

MARIE

have the brains of a male chauvinist pig! Oink! Oink! Oink! Oink! Oink!

LUD

Now who's bein' hateful?

Shh! What was that sound just then?

Sounds like the garage door flapped up! Well, give me them damn glasses.

I see somethin' glowing out there.

Somethin's comin' up the driveway. . . . I never seen anything like it.

AGNUS

Granddaddy Speck . . .

LET! ME! IN!

DAN RATHER
in Skidmore, Texas

TOM BROKAW
in Washington

HARRY REASONER
in Moscow

TRUDY
Everywhere

This is soup
and this is art.
Art.
Soup.
Soup.
Art.
No,
That's Cream of Wheat.
This is soup and this is art.

We must dash soon! We're on our way to Stonehenge. I like to
plan it so we have at least one *peak* experience each day. When
you got aliens in from out of town, you want to do something
special.

It's great traveling with 'em. You go faster than the speed
of speed.

To them, a journey of a thousand miles begins with bio-astral
projection. I said, "*So,* you folks believe in astral projection?"
They said, "If something's true,
you don't need to believe in it."

I'm talkin' *advanced.* They are so advanced they can be
in three different places at once
and still be at one with the universe.

They are so advanced they don't even *try* to prove how advanced
they are. I told 'em we're pretty advanced ourselves. We got
physicists trying to find out more about quarks. They said,
"Trudy, tell your physicists a quark is just one of nature's
little quirks."

They got such a powerful electromagnetic field . . .

just hangin' out with 'em has helped my facial neuralgia.

Only drawback,
I got a severe case of static cling.

They are just about perfect,
except for *one* weak spot:

Their personal appearance. They look like
a gelatinous mass of ribonucleic acid
been poured out of a Jell-O mold too soon.
Plus they got no
eyelids.
That alone would drive *me* up the wall.

We are delving deeply into the history of humanity.

I'm a mound of information.
Yesterday we stumbled across the first recorded history of
when humankind made an ass of itself. Then we discovered
when
humankind first laughed. Guess what!
We first laughed the day we first made an ass of ourselves. They
love that about us!

Right after we laughed, we began to reflect on ourselves.
Around this time we discovered evidence of the first
"knock-knock" joke.
"Knock-knock."
"Who's there?"

"We're not sure—we're new at this."

Not very witty, but it does give us insight into the size and
shape of Cro-Magnon man's funny bone.

I don't know what I'd do without these Post-its. I've got the
facts right at my fingertips. Let me read you some data we found:

- "Did you know, the RNA/DNA molecule can be found throughout
  space in *many* galaxies . . .
  only everybody spells it different?"

- "You *are* what you think."
  Jeez, that's frightening.

- "What goes up must come down.
  But don't expect it to come down
  where you can find it."
  Murphy's Law applied to Newton's.

- "Did you know, in the *entire* universe, we are the only
  intelligent life forms
  thought to have a Miss Universe contest?"

- "Did you know, throughout the cosmos they found intelligent
  life forms that play to play.
  We are the only ones that play to win." Explains why we have
  more than our share
  of losers.

  Oh, they're pretty critical of us, but they said they had to admit
  we're *way* out front
  when it comes to stuff you can make with a blender.

- "Did you know what *most* distinguishes us humans from lower
  animals
  is our desire to take drugs?"

That was for you, Tina.

Nice outfit you barely have on. How's tricks? Pun intended.

You look beautiful, Tina; you smell good. I never know what
drug you're on, but smells like you're *wearing* Opium.
Mind if I sit close?
Mind if I sit *real* close? You mind if I lay down and look up
your nose? You mind if I lay in your lap and take a nap?

TINA

All right now, Trudy, don't mess with me.
I am coasting on my own chemistry and I am
volatile, baby.

I woke up today I felt like I had had *brain surgery* done over
my entire body. I'm thinkin' half the damn day, "What
chemicals did I take to make me feel so wrecked?" Then I
remembered, I hadn't taken *anything*.

Here I was trying to blame a drug for what it feels like to be
straight.

Girl, I am seriously thinking of doing the detox trip again.
I have *never* been so
high as in detox. Those chemicals, before they leave your
bloodstream, baby, they throw *quite* a bon voyage party.

TRUDY

My space chums are very careful what chemicals they put into
their bodies.
Or to use their term, bio-container.

We were havin' a cup of coffee.
I see this strange look come over 'em.
They pointed to the label on this nondairy creamer.
They said, "*Trudy,*
this is *exactly* what we are made of."

L
U
D

Agnus! Turn that junk music *down*! You better learn some manners, young lady, or else . . .

A
G
N
U
S

or else WHAT, Granddaddy Speck?

M
A
R
I
E

Or else people aren't gonna *like* you, honey. You do want to be *liked*, don't you, honey? Everybody wants to be liked.

A
G
N
U
S

NOT ME!
I'M DIF-FER-ENT!

L
U
D

Well, I can't argue with that.

M
A
R
I
E

Lud, do you realize that nothing has turned out the way we planned it?
Not our retirement plan.
Not those Astroturf neckties. "Gonna be such a hit with sports fans, at half time."

Not that cedar closet you built with *artificial* cedar.
The moths just laughed.
Not our patio addition out back,
not our daughter,
and now not our granddaughter.
There's not one thing that panned out right.

LUD
You know what your problem is, Marie?
Too negative. You're negative *about*
ninety-two percent of the time.

MARIE
Yes, and *about* ninety-two percent of the time
I am *dead* right.

LUD
Oh, hell, if you're so damn right all the time, how come we have
a daughter we don't understand too good, and a pink-haired
punk granddaughter got the manners of a terrorist?
Leaves dirty fingerprints on the cheese?
Wears somethin' makes the garage door flap up?

Old man Sanders stopped me today; says he saw somethin' odd-
lookin' in the yard—says it was downright eerie!
Worried we might have poltergeists.

I had to say, "No, that wasn't no poltergeist, that was my
granddaughter.
She glows in the dark 'cause her necklace is a reflective flea
collar."
How do you think that makes me feel?

MARIE

Well, how do you think that makes *me* feel?
Oh, Lud! Why didn't you just go on and let him think it was poltergeists?

Well, speak of the devil!
Agnus, I demand to know where you are going at this time of night looking like that!

AGNUS

YOU! WOULDN'T! WANT TO KNOW!

LUD

Young lady, you tell me where you're going
or you can march that little Day-Glo fanny back in that bedroom and stay there till the paddy wagon comes.

AGNUS

I'm going to a gig, okay?
DON'T WAIT UP!!

MARIE

Lud, look! She has taken the candle out of my good centerpiece. I can't keep anything nice.

LUD

Well, come on to bed. You been stooped over that sewing, got eyes like two cherry tomatoes.

MARIE

You go on to bed. I'm gonna sit up here till she gets back.
Lud . . .

Remember when she was little? She'd stay over. I'd make chocolate milk,

and I'd make me a little milk mustache, and
pretend I didn't notice,
and then you'd make one and there we'd be—the two of us with
little chocolate milk mustaches. Used to just tickle her to death.

You know, she's had a lot to deal with in her short lifetime.

L
U
D

Oh, hell. I've had *more* to deal with in my *long* lifetime. I
don't take it out on the world.

M
A
R
I
E

No, you take it out on *me*.
I called today—
her daddy says they've tried *everything* to get through to her.
They've washed their hands. It's in our laps now.

L
U
D

Well, I bet they haven't tried little milk mustaches. I'll shut that
garage door. When she comes in, we'll hear it flap up.
We'll get up. Have some chocolate milk.
You and me make little milk mustaches,
see if she remembers.

ONSTAGE AT THE UN-CLUB

A
G
N
U
S

I'm getting my act together;
throwing it in your FACE.
I want to insult every member
of the human race. I'm Agnus ANGST.
I don't kiss ass
I don't say thanks.

This will be a night of sharing for the
sharing-impaired. We're all soulmates, after all,
in the vast cosmic dustbin of intergalactic space.
The universe contains at least
one hundred billion galaxies, each galaxy contains at least
one hundred billion stars, and we are
micro-SPECKS
on SPECK-ship earth.

So the fact that my
parents kicked me out of the house
and someone stole my parakeet
should mean very little in the scheme of things, but
"No, I am *quite* UPSET about IT."

T V "To boldly go where no 'punk' has gone before.
V O Suburbia!"
I
C
E

A As I was leaving to come to the Un-Club tonight,
G my grandmother speck said,
N "As long as you're going out, take out the trash."
U
S

I look around the room. I see her seashells shadow box and her
lima bean and split pea mosaic and decoupage
hanging over granddaddy speck's Berkline recliner rocker, the
kind they give away on game shows.
I see her imitation Early American maple coffee table
in the shape of a
wagon wheel.
I see her salt and pepper shaker collection on the
simu–Early American knickknack shelf.
I see this wrought-iron lamppost with this
ceramic drunk
leaning against it.
I see it, but I don't believe it.
Take out the *trash*? I wanted to say,
"I wouldn't know where to begin."

T V "And *these*
V O are the *days*
I of our *lives*."
C
E

A G N U S

What's coming up for me is something from my own soap opera.

I look at my family,
I feel like a detached retina.

The last really deep conversation I had with my dad
was between our T-shirts. His said "Science Is Truth Found
Out." Mine said "The Truth Can Be Made Up If You Know How."

Even as a fetus, I had womb angst. Inside the amniotic sac,
the fetus has this headset
that is plugged into this DNA tape loop
that plays
over and over, auto-reverse, all the rotten things
that have happened throughout
history.

I knew the world I was coming into was liable to be a
tampered-with-Tylenol, pins-in-girl-scout-cookies, ground-
zero kind of place.

I wanted *everything* to be perfect. What's coming up for me
is my dinner.

T V   **V O I C E**

"And *these*
are the *days*
of our *lives.*"

A G N U S

On the radio, I heard the weatherman say,

"The air today is unacceptable. People with breathing problems
should not go out."

I wanted to shout,
"What's unacceptable
is that the *air* is unacceptable!"
I think: Wow, breathing is a bio-hazard.

If we don't take in air every few minutes, we die,
but the air we are taking in
is killing us.

I rush to my Behavior Modification Center, hoping they can
help me
cut down on my habit
of *breathing.*

In the cubicle next to mine I hear: "Do you want to stop
drinking?"
"No."
"Do you want to stop *smoking?*"
"No."
"Do you want to stop *overeating?*"
"No. I want to stop caring
that I eat and drink and smoke too much!"

Flash: New Marketing Business Venture: Start behavior-
modification-type religion
where people can go to learn to stop caring.

(That's the music cue, you techno-nerd!
That's it, now turn up the volume, louder, louder—that's better.)

THE CANDELIGHT SERVICE IS
ABOUT TO BEGIN
ANYONE WHO WANTS TO
IS WELCOME TO COME IN

DE BOBINE

" *'Cause you*
Light up my life.
You give me hope
To carry on.
You light up my days
And fill my nights
with song."

I want to share something vital
I just read in this self-help book
I took from the trash can
in the ladies' room at the
House of Pancakes.
Will, by G. Gordon Liddy,
Master of the Watergate caper.

My new guru.
Who, when holding his hand
over a lit candle, said,
"The trick is not to mind it."

And I don't mind it
when I first came into
this world
Elvis was already fat.

And I didn't mind it
when I heard that Ozzy Osbourne
bit the head
off a bat.

I don't mind
I was born
at the time of the crime
known as Watergate.

And must've missed out
on most things
that made America great.
But I don't mind it.

And I don't mind
no matter how much contempt
I have for society
it's nothing compared
to the contempt
society has for me.

I don't mind
that the phrase "truth in advertising"
was probably just some lie
thought up by some guy
in advertising.

I don't mind that
there's no more avant-garde
(but my mom took it pretty hard).

I used to be proud
I stuck out from the crowd
now everyone's marching
to a different drummer
what a bummer!
But *I* don't mind it.

I don't mind that I took my goldfish
and I put it in water
from the faucet
and it died;
our drinking water
caused it.

I tried my mouth-to-mouth
resuscitation skills.
My dad said, "*You* are the
daughter of a scientist;
it should've been
mouth-to-gills."
But I don't mind it.

I don't mind
each morning I get up
I feel like I want to vomit.

I don't mind that
the teenage suicide rate
is soaring
like Halley's comet.

The boy in school
that I loved the most
died last year of an overdose.
But I don't mind it.

I have set as my goal
to get so strong
I could peel onions
all day long
and never shed one tear—

I want my skin to thicken
so if I am panic-stricken
when post-nuke day gets here
I won't even feel the fear
as I watch me and the world disappear.

The trick is not to mind it—
if you're looking for peace
this is where you'll find it.

Gordon Liddy showed me the way:
I have been on
heavy metaphor maintenance
all day.

For life
is like that candle flame
and we
are like Gordon Liddy's hand
hovering
over it.

And it hurts
like hell,

but the trick

is not

to mind it.

A
G
N
U
S

I MIND IT!!

PART II

Excuse me while I fluff up. My space chums are due any minute.

We're having drinks with Richard Leakey. Settle some questions that we got about evolution.

They asked *me*, was man still looking for the missing link?

I told *them*, "I thought man *was* the missing link."

They think, like me:

If evolution was worth its salt,
by now it should've evolved something better than
survival of the fittest. Yeah, I told 'em I think
a better idea would be survival of the
wittiest. At least, that way,
the creatures that didn't survive could've died *laughing*.
You'd think by now evolution could've at least evolved us to the
place where we could change
ourselves.

Seems like
evolution has just kinda plateaued out,
left mankind with a middle management problem.

Or maybe evolution's got burnout. Or *maybe* evolution figures
it'll let the bio-engineers do the work for a change.

For a long time now, it appears we've been a species
on auto-snooze.

My space chums think my unique hookup with
humanity could be
evolution's awkward attempt to jump-start itself up again.

They're thinking just maybe, going crazy could be the
evolutionary process trying to hurry up mind expansion.

Maybe my mind didn't snap. Maybe it was just trying to stretch
itself
into a new shape.
The cerebral cortex trying to grow a thumb of sorts.

It might seem like I got delusions of grandeur on top of
everything else, but maybe I didn't have a
breakdown—maybe I had a break*through*. Maybe
evolution's using my mind in some kind of scientific
experiment.

Sure feels like it.
But look, if I can be of service to humankind's progress, the
loss of my mind is a small price to pay.
I just think I should have been consulted.

My space chums are concerned about our evolvement
because they say we're all connected.
"Everything is part of everything."
They started talking about a little something they call
"interstellar interspecies symbiosis." To hold up my end of
the conversation, I asked them to
elaborate.

So they brought up the Quantum Inseparability Principle.
"Every particle affects every other particle everywhere."

They tried to bring quantum physics down to a level I could more clearly
misunderstand. Then one of them mentioned the Bootstrap Theory, and at the point they got into the Superstring Theory, frankly, I think even *they* were in over their heads.
But here's what I got from it all:

Seems like there's some kind of cosmic Krazy Glue connecting everything to everything.

We all time-share the same atoms. "There is only one sky."
"That which is above is also in that which is below."
"What is there is also here." So said the Upanishads.

But the question remains, "Where the *hell* are the Upanishads?"
Come to think of it, I don't know where *Leakey* is, either.

Oh, here come my space chums now, late as usual.
I've been waiting for you guys. Listen, I think we'll scratch Leakey;
I'm really all you need. Besides, too many cooks spoil the soup.

Soup!

This is soup and this is art! Art! Soup! Soup! Art!

Uh-oh, thunder!
Quick, it's gonna pour! Put up your umbrella hats . . .

and follow me.

Hi, Tina. Hi, Brandy.
Keep a sharp eye out—
the fuzz is buzzin' the nabe tonight.

BRANDY

Tina, Tina, hurry. Hurry, Tina, he wants you, too!

Quick, get in the backseat.

Hey. Hey, you're not a trick. What are you? A writer?
Tina, tape recorder. Another writer type.
Everybody's doing an article on
the life. You're lucky you got me; I got so many stories
you won't have to interview no one else.

Drive up Ninth.
You're the second guy this month wants to take out trade in
this bizarre fashion. Last one was more normal. He ended up
wantin' my life history
and a blowjob.

What you said before—you wasn't interested what's between my
legs, huh?

Just my life history?

TINA

I got news. What's between her legs
is her life history. But me and Brandy are gettin'
out of this genital jive; we got entrepreneurial
plans . . .
telephone sex . . .
reach millions. Yeah, that's the wave of the
future. No germs and no
hand-to-hand combat. 'Cause eventually,
it could be any day now, people are not gonna want
to take the chance to go out.

When we get around the block,
let's stop for a chocolate soda;
I got the craves for something sweet.

Brandy, look at that pitiful scrawny punk kid. . . .

Hey, you skinny teenybopper punkette! Get off the streets
and go back to school!

She won't be no good at hookin', all punked out like that.
All the dudes I've talked with say the punk thing
makes 'em go limp.
And she oughta choose *one* color for her hair
and stick with it.

BRANDY

What'd she call us, Tina? Some kind of "speck"?
That baby brat ain't in the life—not yet. She's just another
runaway. But in a few weeks, she'll be *all* different . . .
Ever see a stray *dog* on the streets? I can tell just like *that*
which ones will survive and which ones won't. I don't know how
I can tell but I can tell. Right, Tina?

Like there was this dog Princess, belonged to this
ol' wino dude Jim.
Delivered take-outs for this Greek place over on Eighth. Lunch
hour they put him through the ringer . . . take this to 1650
Broadway . . . take that to the Brill . . . go here, go there . . . 'cause
everyone loves
that eggplant and grape leaves. Notorious. Him and Princess—
like Siamese twins.

Fade out, fade in. Jim gets so stressed out one lunch hour, he just
keels over in a hump like that.

TINA

You put too much stress on the human body, baby, it simply
rebels. *Tell* me about it.

BRANDY

Long story short: paramedics come, they announce him dead as
a doornail, pour him into one of those plastic body bags. You
know, like a Hefty only for dead people. The paramedics quick
toss Jim in the ambulance, then run, jump in, start the motor.
Princess sees 'em moving out with Jim inside, now she freaks,
howlin' and yowlin', she all of a sudden jerks herself loose and
tears out after 'em.

Fade out, fade in. They're takin' the body bag out of the
ambulance . . . when . . .

T
I
N
A
Girl, girl, let *me* tell the rest. This dog with her bony ass,
she runs up to the body bag, she starts whinin' and scratchin'.
She gets the bag open, starts lickin' Jim's face, and
that old wino he all of a sudden pops up out the bag like an old
rusty bedspring. Well, baby, those medics just about had *heart
failure* theyselves.

B
R
A
N
D
Y
But they make Jim go inside for a checkup, 'cause even though,
true, he's not dead . . .

T
I
N
A
Still he don't look all that *well,* either.

B
R
A
N
D
Y
Fade in, fade out.
Nobody around here ever sees Jim again.
Maybe he died, maybe he didn't.
None of us couldn't be sure.
We didn't know his last name. Hospital's notorious for bad
records, anyway, so even if *we'd* known his last name and
even his mother's maiden name, the hospital might still
have drawn a blank.

T
I
N
A
Some people surmise it's *always* such a long wait,
maybe he died in the waiting room.
I am convinced what did it was being stuffed into a body bag
while he was still alive. He came to,
he thought:
Body bag.
I must be dead.
And the thought that he was dead
could be the very thing that killed him.

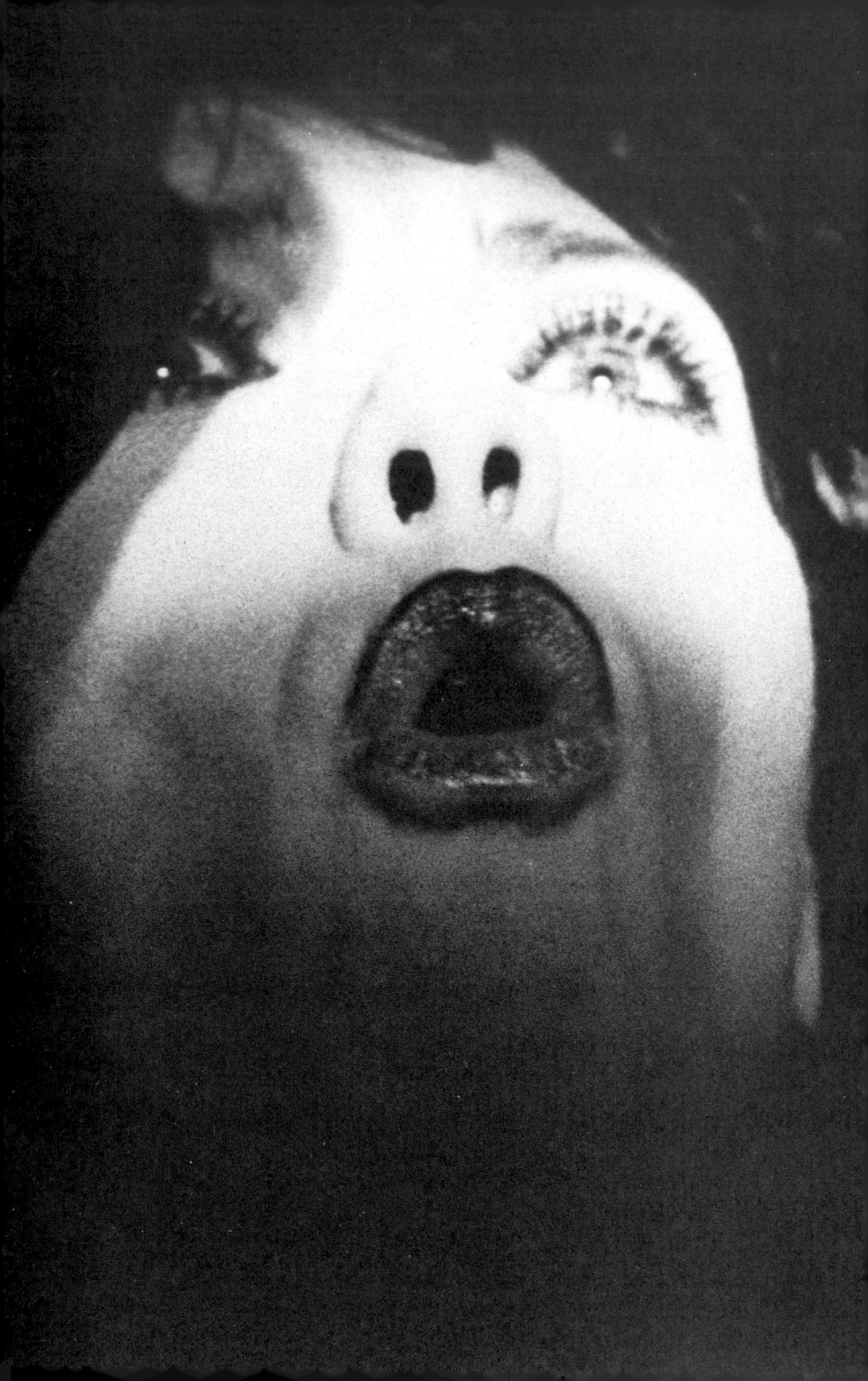

The mind is a powerful tool.
I think when something happens to somebody to that drastic
extent, I think it must be astrological. Haven't you had days when
things go so wrong,
there's just no other explanation?

BRANDY
Anyway, fade out, fade in.
Next day on the corner I see Princess. Shakin'.
Like I never saw her before.
She don't know what hit her. That's the look on her face.
She just knows the wino's not there. The look they get on
their face when they give up, I know. I know that look.
I said to myself, "This dog is not gonna last out here." Sure
enough, she didn't, and it wasn't she lacked for food, Tina, the
Greeks fed her, I checked.

TINA
Yeah, but what kind of food is that for a dog—
grape leaves and baklava?

BRANDY
She just never kicked into that survival mode like you need to—
to survive—like you and me did, Tina—
you either do or you don't.

Here, slow down.

TINA
Well, don't you ever let 'em put *me* into a body bag, Brandy,
unless you prepared to catch that ambulance, rip that bag open
and lick my face, 'cause I don't have no pet to
look out for me.

BRANDY
Pull over.

Hey, Trudy. Trudy. Run inside Howard Johnson's, get Tina a
chocolate soda,
yourself fried clams. Don't get wet.

TINA

But you know, the tune that keeps playin' over in my mind:
That dog had the dumbest look on her face, but she was smart
enough to know Jim was alive, which was more than you can say
for us!
The medics, too. And life and death is their expertise. That dog
knew *some*thing about life didn't none of *us* know.

BRANDY

That dog. You can't say that dog knew more about life
than *us,* Tina. It's just that she knew somethin' more about . . .
Jim.

We know about life. While you're writin' about life,
we're out here on the streets living life on a gut-level basis.
I could be a shrink. I should hang out a shingle.
People tell me things. Forget it. Things they don't even tell to
people they're close to, *especially* to people they're close
to, because . . .

I don't know, they'd be too embarrassed maybe, I guess,
but they tell me
because I swear people don't want sex so much as they want
somebody
who'll listen to 'em about, I don't know, their problems,
you know.
People don't need sex so much as they need to be listened to.
People don't realize that's the secret of our business.

TINA

Yeah, that's the first thing you learn after fellatio
is how to listen.

BRANDY

Can the vulgarity! We've got a sensitive writer here.
One time a bunch of us was doin' a stroll around the waterfront. This
guy shows up, sensitive type, soft . . .
type of guy I go for. He just wants to talk. Talks to me not like
I'm a prostitute; he talks to me like I'm his . . . I don't know,
sister, maybe.
Fade out, fade in. Turns out he don't know what to do with his
life . . . he's thinkin' maybe he'd do some hustlin', put himself
through beauty school,
which was an ambition he had, only where would he get the
money, right?
So he's askin' me would I give him some pointers on the life?
You know, wise him up and all.

TINA

Girl, you're too open with people.
It's one thing tellin' about Jim, Jim's dead, but . . .

BRANDY

I'm not gonna tell his real name, don't worry.

So we're walkin' across the pier to this bar when this car
pulls up and this guy yells, "Hey, sweetie, could I get a ferry
here?" I go over to the car, I come back, and
the kid's standing there
with this look on his face
like if you was to see right before your very eyes, all at
once, every sad movie that was ever made. This is the look he
had.
I said, "Bucci, what's wrong?"

Oh, Tina . . . I said his name.

Turns out he thinks the guy was makin' fun of him, see, makin'
a crack, you know, "ferry"—"fairy." He was gay, and it hurt
him. 'Cause inside he had a lot of unfinished business.
I told him the guy really wanted directions to the Staten

Island ferry—that there was no reason to feel so hurt. He starts
tellin' me his whole life story.
How he could never do nothin' right . . . how his macho he-man
father once caught him wearin' his mom's
bathing suit. And he describes the shame he felt. And I said,
"Like the shame you felt just now?"
And he just nodded.
And I told him the only thing he should be ashamed of
is being ashamed.

Yeah, I should hang out a shingle.
People's insecurities! I *tell* ya. Him on the streets? No way, I told
him. He
wouldn't last three weeks. He'd go the way of Princess.

Fade out, fade in. I end up stakin' him to beauty school. The
deal, in return he pays me back when he can, which he did, and
for interest he would have to do my hair free for the rest of my
life.
My hair, don't ask. I didn't have split ends.
I had split roots. But now . . .

here, feel, don't be shy, feel. Isn't it soft and shiny? I mean,
beauty school, it's not like he was gonna be a cardiologist,
right?

Fade in, fade out. He is now *the* top hair stylist at a
certain Fifth Avenue salon which shall be nameless, but if we
cross to
Fifth and drive by Trump's I could show it to you.

T
I
N
A

Brandy, we gotta get back, meet that telephone dude.

BRANDY

Oh, yeah. Listen, Bucci's real name must not be used.
Or mine.
You swear? Come on, swear.
But when you're talkin' about me, I do want to know. I know,
why don't
you call me "the girl with the exquisite hair." Then I'll
know. Pull over, we'll get out here.

Watch it gettin' out, Tina.
Don't step in that big puddle.
Ciao!

TINA

Brandy, you're too open with people. If you noticed, I held back.
I'm not selling the screenplay to my life for no fifty dollars.
We could get a tape recorder.
We can be writers, too.
You don't need to know how to type no more.
We can write as good as he can write if what he's writing is
what we're talking. We should've got co-credit, or something.

When that article comes out, it's gonna say,
Written by him.

It should at least say,
Lived by Brandy and Tina.

BRANDY

Tina, I forgot to ask him what magazine he's writin' for.

TINA

Yeah, be just our damn luck, we could get famous and not even
know it. Fade in, fade out, baby.

HOWARD JOHNSON'S, FORTY-SIXTH AND BROADWAY

TRUDY

Chocolate soda. Side of clams. I got money. Hey, and make it snappy, Howard.

I got a big night planned for my space chums.
Should be a peak experience: violin concert, all kids.
Howard, you mind if I spread out here on the counter? I gotta get these Post-its collated. My secretary's out sick. Everywhere I look, Post-its. I got Post-its comin' out of my ear. I must collate my notes. As per usual, we came out of our last meeting more confused than ever.

They started asking me a lot of deep questions
about God, movies, you name it.

"Did Adam have a navel?" "Was it a innie or a outie?"

Let me read you some of our latest findings:

- We think Peking Man may be even more advanced than we originally thought. Not only did we discover bones and ashes which prove he cooked his meat, but we also found traces of what appears to be
  barbecue sauce.

- When a person dies of thirst, their eyes tear up.

- When a man gets hanged, he gets an erection, but when a woman gets hanged, the *last* thing on her mind
  is sex.

- Here's another: As soon as humankind began to discover the truth about itself, we began to find ways
  to cover up that truth. But maybe that's for the best: Our ability to delude ourselves may be an important
  survival tool.

Some of this stuff we find I'd just as soon not know. We got new
evidence as to what motivated man to walk upright: to free his
hands for masturbation.

We did some studies, Howard. We're still working on when
superficiality began showing up in human nature.
Nothin' in our studies gives us a clear picture as to the chain of
events that must've taken place.
We can only speculate. At one point, Howard,
we were hunters and gatherers and then seems like, all of a
sudden, we became
partygoers.

We speculated what it was like before we got language skills:
When we humans had our first thought, most
likely we didn't know what to think. It's hard to think
without words 'cause you haven't got a clue as to what you're
thinking. So if you think we suffer from a lack of communication
now,
think what it must've been like then, when people lived in a
verbal void—
made worse by the fact that there were no words such as
"verbal void."

They figure language happened maybe something like this.
One day man was walking along barefoot
as they did in those days, and suddenly stubbed his toe.
He said, "Ouch." Then he must've thought: Gee, I wonder what I
meant by that?
Pretty soon he felt his toe *throbbing* and he knew
the meaning of "ouch." When primitive man had his "ouch"
experience, Howard, he couldn't have known he was paving the
way years later for Helen Keller to have her "wa-wa"
experience.

I personally think we
developed language because of our deep inner need
to complain.

Right after we started talking to each other we began to talk
behind each other's backs. Sometimes it was vicious gossip,
other times a casual critical remark, like "Jeez, did you see
the hair on his back?" When it dawned on everybody that not
only could they talk,
but they could also be talked *about,*
primitive man began showing signs of
paranoia. With everyone so paranoid, war soon broke out.
With war came stress, and the rest is history.

My space chums are really quite concerned about the Stress
Factor we're so susceptible to. They worry about us. They even
worry more than that
actress on stage at the Plymouth Theater.
They said to me, "Trudy, beyond any bio-force we have ever
encountered, Human Nature is the most thought-stirring, neuro-
numbing, heart-boggling of all.

They say just as the whole chemistry of the ocean
can be found in each drop of sea water,
all the profound emotional polarities of Human Nature are
crammed into each bio-container—or, to use our term, human
body.

It could be just *too* much for any one
bio-container to grapple with.

Frankly, I think *they're* showing signs of stress, too. Hard to deal
with their mood swings. Lately, I've been walking on eggs
'cause the least little thing can set 'em off on a crying jag.
I think they may be getting too emotionally involved with us.
They keep wanting me to dial-switch back to certain people so
they can see what happened to them. I think
the bonding thing might be happening.

We're *all* overworked; I just don't know how long we
can keep up this pace.

Something they said the other day gave me a pang—
makes me wonder if they're thinking of leaving here.
They said they wanted to pick up a few souvenirs and some
postcards.
So we went to some shops around Broadway, and frankly,
I was embarrassed for my species. Everything was in such
bad taste. But they understand.
They said, "Earth is a planet still in its puberty." In fact,
from their planet,
Earth looks like it has pimples.

I did have some I♡MANKIND T-shirts made up, but something
in their electromagnetic field caused the fabric to
demolecularize, if that's the word.

So I'm still lookin' for suitable souvenirs.
I hate to think of them going,
but frankly, all this data leaves us with more questions
than answers. It's a back-breaking task just collating all this info,
not to mention trying to make sense out of it.

Here's one that gave me pause:
- "Did you know Weltschmerz exists throughout the universe?"

I turned to 'em point-blank and asked 'em,
"Okay, you've learned a lot about us
but tell me this, and be honest:
what do you think of people
as a whole?"

They said they thought it would be
a excellent idea.
Hey, Howard, when Tina comes in give her the soda and the rest
of my clams.
I must dash soon.
Almost time for the concert.
You know how I like to impress 'em with all the
miraculous stuff we humans are capable of.

Tonight we're gonna see a bunch of little kids playing
violin. If that doesn't impress 'em, I'll eat
my umbrella hat.

One peak experience coming up!
Uh-oh, irregular brain activity. Static white noise . . .

Now where am I? . . .
Reception coming in strong . . . Looks like a yard sale . . .
See boxes, price tags, toys . . . People milling around . . .
There's a woman packing up books.
She takes the last one, *Free to Be You and Me,*
and puts it into a box.
People go over, ask her questions:
Where's the top to this?
How much is this? This is cracked; what about a dollar off?
Does this work? Where's the cord to the toaster?
Is this for sale? . . .

GARAGE SALE, LOS ANGELES, 1985

L   How could anyone accumulate so much junk?
Y

N   No, I still have to go through those tapes, but everything on
this side of the yard is for sale. *Those?* Those are the twins'
Bataca encounter bats. You can have those for nothing.
And these Geraldine Ferraro buttons.
Yes, the water bed goes too. There must be a price tag
somewhere.
This? Oh, look at this.
My journal. I've been looking everywhere for it.

FROM LYN'S JOURNAL, 1970, N.Y.C.

> The "Women's Strike for Equality" march.
> I taped all the speeches—Kate Millett, Bella Abzug—
> but nothing came out clear except Betty Friedan saying:
> > "We, today . . . have learned
> > the *power* of our Sisterhood!"
> And we did! I'm so glad we made the trip—even though at times
> I didn't think we were going to make it in Edie's
> old VW. It was worth risking our lives. I think the only thing that
> kept that old junkheap moving was Edie singing
> "Ain't No Mountain High Enough"
> at the top of her lungs.
>
> We've been on a high since we got here. Giddy, in fact.
> But I can't wait to get back to L.A. We're going to form
> a consciousness-raising group just like
> thousands of women all over the country are doing.

FROM LYN'S JOURNAL, 1971

I can't believe Henry Kissinger actually said
"Power is the ultimate aphrodisiac." I loved Edie's comment:
"The bombing in Vietnam shows what it takes for *him* to get it up!"
Women don't want to fight. As Marge says,
"We'd rather sit around in a circle and process."
I really feel when women get equality—
social and economic equality—
there'll be no more wars.
This is about moving the *whole* species forward,
not just half of it.

A CONSCIOUSNESS-RAISING GROUP, LOS ANGELES, 1972

LYN   Sisters! Progress report:

"Boy Scouts of America allow girls into its
Explorer Scouts division!"

EDIE   *"Ain't no mountain high enough."*

L Y N	"Girls are appointed as Senate pages for the first time in history!"
E D I E	Make that "herstory."
L Y N	And oh, is this a breakthrough, or what? Since 1920, the Big Ten has had only men in their marching bands during football season. This season the University of Minnesota has decided to let women march with the men during football games.
M A R G E	What more could you want? *I am Woman, hear me roar.*
L Y N	*"Oh, thank you, University of Minnesota. Being just a majorette was sapping my 'woman-strength.' "* And, Sisters, I've got a surprise. *Ms.* magazine. Premier issue! Look, I got Gloria Steinem herself to autograph them. Here's yours, Edie, for you, Marge, and this one is for me.

A NEIGHBORHOOD HANGOUT, 1973

THE JUKEBOX: AL GREEN, "LET'S STAY TOGETHER"

EDIE

Let's have champagne! This is a night for celebration.
Not only did the Sisters get to watch Billy Jean
bust Bobby Riggs's chauvinistic butt
but guess what? I got a job at *The Free Press* doing my
own feature:
"Boycotts of the Month"!

MARGE

Well, it sounds like we got our own West Coast
Jill Johnston. You're lucky you got a job at that kind of place
—now you won't have to give up those
camouflage fatigues you love so much.
I mean, honey, you couldn't *be* more antiwar,
but if it weren't for army surplus
you'd have *nothing* to wear.
Lyn, I'm not exaggerating. Edie was in my plant store yesterday
in those camouflage overalls.
I almost watered her.

LYN

Okay, are you two going to rib each other all night or can we get
down to some real issues.

EDIE

I'm proud that I've never been a slave to the tyranny of
fashion trends, like you, Marge.

MARGE

Unless camouflage fatigues, political rhetoric and
boycotts of the month could be called
fashion trends.

E
D
I
E

Marge, your problem is
your role models
were models.

L
Y
N

Edie, you and I should only have Marge's taste in clothes.

E
D
I
E

Oh, Marge has great taste in everything,
except when it comes to men. Marge,
the "Lib" in Women's Lib stands for liberation, not
libido.
I mean, what good is it, Sis, to have sexual freedom
if you become a slave to it? You've got *Cosmo* damage.
You should boycott those women's magazines and start
reading my column.

L
Y
N

At least Marge has figured out from those women's magazines
what shape face she has, Edie—
something *I've* never been sure of.

E
D
I
E

So she can apply makeup to overcome flaws? If your face is oval,
they tell you to make it square. If it's square,
they tell you to make it longer. Sometimes you make it too long
and got to make it square again
which was how you looked at the start
only now you got a square face that's too made up where before
you had a nice natural-looking square face. I don't care if I got
the cheekbones of an
isosceles triangle or the forehead of a Pithecanthropus.
I look at myself and I don't see any flaws;
that's what these consciousness-raising
self-examinations are all about.

CONSCIOUSNESS-RAISING SESSION

MARGE
Okay, Edie, you say you don't see any flaws,
but I'm looking at my breasts,
I'm looking at Lyn's—and
they do not point upwards like they're "supposed to."

LYN
Marge, I just don't give a shit anymore.

EDIE
Hey, and mine aren't big enough to point in any
direction, and I never did give a shit,
and who says we need to shave under our arms?
Ta-dah!

MARGE
Oh, no! What is that—Spanish moss? How did you *manage* that
much growth? I mean, the Women's Movement is still *young.*

EDIE
Your plant food, Marge . . . and a Gro-Lite.

LYN
Body hair! A sure way to tell the radicals from the
middle-of-the-roaders, like me.
*May*be I could let hair grow a few days on my legs, but under
the *arms*? Edie, you're probably on some FBI list of the
politically dangerous;

ON THE PHONE

L
Y
N

Edie is becoming more radical by the minute, Marge.
Today we had lunch at this restaurant. She had on a tank top, she
leaned back, and I saw one armpit as smooth-shaven as a
bathing suit model, and in the other armpit, this
shock of hair. I'm not sure *what* it meant politically,
but it *did* have visual impact.

FROM LYN'S JOURNAL, 1974

I don't know what Edie wants. She thinks Marge and I are too
middle-of-the-road, and maybe we are. But I have marched and
rallied till I'm *bleary*-eyed. For Shirley Chisholm. For
Bella. I've licked so many envelopes, my tongue has paper cuts.
I'm just going to have to tell her I'm sorry about the
Jo Ann Little thing, but I promised Peter I'd go skiing and I'm
keeping that promise.
I cannot be what Edie wants and still
be all Peter needs me to be.

Edie's right when she says Peter's suppressive.
He is.
But no more so than Edie (I'd like to tell her).
Why do I always put myself in a place where I'm trying to
please people who seem impossible to please?
I saw a *Mary Tyler Moore* rerun tonight,
and I couldn't help seeing how much I'm like Mary,
and Peter is self-involved like Ted Knight,
and Edie is just like Lou Grant.
I must work on this with Dr. Stein.
Glad I finally made an appointment—only wish I'd
been in therapy *long* before now.

AT THE THERAPIST'S

L
Y
N

So, Doctor, we started fighting on the ski lift and Peter let
slip he didn't think a woman could make a good President and
that the feminist movement was making a monster of me.

It was the worst fight we ever had.
He said Edie was poisoning my mind.
That my CR sessions were making me conscious of everything
but his dissatisfaction with the relationship.
And he said . . . and this is what really hurt . . .
he said that I *used* to be so sexy, but now I'd even lost
my sex appeal.

I bolted off that ski lift so mad. Halfway down, I slammed
smack into a pine stump. I know he saw it, but he skied right
past me.

Okay, Doctor, but Gestalt therapy is new to me.
In this chair, I role-play Peter; in this chair, I role-play
myself, right? And in that chair,
you role-play the doctor?

"Peter, I am sick of this suppressive, you-do-as-I-say macho
number you have been putting me through."

Now I'm me. No, I'm Peter. "And I'm sick of this
suppressive feminist trip you've been dumping on me."

Doctor, who said that? Is this Peter's chair?

"I'd like a *glimpse* of the nurturant female you and your
butch/rad/fem friends harp on so much. I want a woman,
not a feminist!"

"Ah ha! All it is with you is sex, sex, sex!"

"And all it is with you is sex, sex,
sexual politics! I have *had* it!"

I don't know exactly *what* happened, Doctor,
but I feel like I've just walked out on myself.

THE NEXT SESSION

L
Y
N

Then, Doctor, I went to this Holly Near concert.
I saw Edie waving me over . . . she looked so *different*.

She was wearing Indian cotton drawstring pants,
Birkenstock sandals
and a "Sisters of Silkwood" T-shirt. She introduced me to her
friend Pam. She's clearly into a new phase.

And then someone very attractive came over, passing out
candles. An artist from the Woman's Building, Janet.

She was wearing Indian cotton drawstring pants,
Birkenstock sandals
and a "Lesbians Ignite" T-shirt. She'd made the candles
herself.

Not the usual phallic-shaped.

They were formed like a . . . a beautiful labia majora.

The wick, Edie pointed out,
symbolized a tampon string.

The evening took a strange turn.
Maybe it was my breakup with Peter or maybe I just felt like
widening the parameters of my sexuality.

I guess I should tell everything, right, Doctor?
Well, Janet turned out to be a regular "Don Juanita."
She *loves* to make love, and when *she* gets tired she has an old
vibrator that heats up to such an extent I have to get up, go into
the kitchen and get an oven mitt.

She's a multimedia performance artist,
heavy into video documents. Her latest art piece,
Life Imitates the Avant-Garde,
earned her a paragraph in *Chrysalis.*

THE NEXT SESSION

L
Y
N

She's making a docu-diary of our relationship . . .
she tapes *everything*
and now she's putting me
in her performance-art pieces.

Last night she put white greasepaint on my face,
draped me in gauze veils,
put on a John Cage tape
and I had to sit in a downtown gallery
on a stack of Harvard Classics
while dazed art patrons milled around me,
cocking their heads this way and that,
whispering to each other about
what it all meant.
I said to her, "Janet, no one, including me, knows what's
going on."
But she says that was the whole point—
that *my* not knowing
and no one *else* knowing
was what it was all about.
She makes me feel so . . . so . . . *linear.*
See, her theory is if *no* one knows
what it's about, it might jolt us out of our normal
mode of perceiving,

and in having *no* information whatsoever,
we'd be forced to confront *new* information. . . .

Of course, Edie cut through it all;
she looked Janet straight in the eye and said,
"New information about what . . . ?"

I sat for forty minutes under the veils
and then Janet's little five-year-old, Agnus, came in
carrying a candle, which, for reasons known only to Janet,
was burning at both ends.
I took the candle
and that's when my veil caught on fire.
I grabbed Agnus up,
trying to protect her, but she ran away.
I swear she was worried we'd
ruined her mother's performance piece.

AT THE GALLERY

L
Y
N
Marge, how come no one lifted a finger to help?

M
A
R
G
E
Frankly, honey, we were confused. We thought it could've been
part of the act. But I loved it. Daniel loved
it. We all *loved* it.

E
D
I
E
Hey, Marge, let's face it, Sis, since you fell
in love with Disco Danny over there, you love
everything.

AT THE THERAPIST'S

L   The evening ended in total chaos, Doctor.
Y   We hear fire trucks. Suddenly firemen were everywhere.
N   Agnus had called them to put out the veil.
Patrons were fleeing the gallery.
Janet got the whole thing on video, including our
breakup.
And I asked her to dub me off a copy.

Two suppressive relationships in a row have put me
under a lot of stress, Doctor, and frankly, this
therapy is stressful all on its own. I'm thinking
of trying TM. It won't interfere with our sessions,
will it?

ANOTHER SESSION, 1975

L   I met somebody, Doctor....
Y
N   I'm at the TM center in Santa Monica waiting to
get my mantra
and I meet this really great-looking guy
who's waiting to have *his* mantra checked.
He was wearing Indian cotton drawstring pants,
Birkenstock sandals
and a T-shirt that said "Whales Save Us."

I liked him right off. He has kind of a, I don't know, a post-
psychedelic air about him like somebody who
maybe in college one time had read Gurdjieff
or the Tibetan Book of the Dead
on acid.
We split to this vegetarian place nearby, the Golden Temple.
I had something that tasted like a tofu melt.
Talking with him was such a high.
He *listens* with an intensity most other people have only when
talking. Doctor, I knew he was "getting" me on so
many different levels. He could just look at me
and it was like I could feel all my
chakras opening.
I remember our exact conversation—word for word.
I felt so totally comfortable talking about myself—

I know it may not seem so to you, but it's
not something I do that easily—I mean, I find I'm
not that open with most people, not really. That's why I keep
a journal, I guess.

I told him I have a master's in Art History, but I realized too
late it didn't exactly insure my future.
So I'm getting a degree in marketing.
Out of high school,
I'd gone to art school, but somewhere along the way
I developed creative block. Then later I worked in
a gallery where they sold all this terrible art and
I realized that some people
when they develop creative block
may be doing the world a favor.

He laughed at that, then he told me he was building
a Samadhi flotation tank, that I should use it
when he finished it because it was good for creative
blocks. He invited me to his place.

I told him I'd love to another time,
but that I had my shift on the Rape Crisis Hot Line.
Then he asked about the weekend;
I told him I had my est training,
and we got up to leave.
Then the funniest thing happened—I looked down, and
realized I had picked up Bob's bag
and he'd picked up mine.
We *even* have the same taste in shoulder bags!

And I split, my heart was pounding.
The herb tea had been caffeine-free.
If it wasn't the tea, what was happening to me?

Oh, Doctor, remember, this will have to be our last session
for a while. I'm not supposed to be in therapy when I'm in est.

AT THE NEIGHBORHOOD HANGOUT

LYN   Next to you, Edie, Bob is the truest feminist I've ever met.
He's the only man I've ever known who knew where he was
when Sylvia Plath died.

He has a master's in Business, but what changed his life: he
read *The Wall Street Journal* on acid.

Bob has this dream: to be a holistic
capitalist.

EDIE   Well, I'll believe this Prince Charming when I see him.

MARGE   How come I never meet a guy like that?

EDIE   Because you go to the discos instead of the TM center, Marge.

MARGE   You're right. The last guy I went to bed with, I woke up in
the morning, I practically had the imprint of his coke spoon on
my chest.

EDIE   You have "heterosexual damage," Sis. I mean, all that
Ortho-Novum is bound to seep into your bloodstream.

FROM LYN'S JOURNAL, 1975

In the hallway, outside his apartment, I heard New Age music.
I smelled musk-scented candles. When he opened the door, his
face was flushed; I knew that he'd just come down from his
anti-gravity boots. . . .

We talked about est. I joked and told him
I got several things. I got whatever you get even if
you're not sure what it is you got or even that you
got it, then that's what you're *supposed* to get.

I also got that he was the kind of person I could share what I
got *with* . . . even if we weren't sharing it
in bed.

Bob showed me the Samadhi isolation tank and then I stretched
out on his water bed.

He gave me a shiatsu massage.

He knew I had seminar stiffness.

We smoked some paraquat-free Panama Red and then
we made love.

Afterwards, we talked into the night. Bob poured
out all his feelings about things that concerned him:
megavitamin therapy, solar energy, the ecosystem
and ending world hunger through tofu consciousness.

We made love again. And then stopped and had a Trail Mix
snack.

We talked till dawn, exchanging Patti Hearst theories, and then
we fell asleep.

By morning we were in love. Bob is a dream come true . . .
a New Age Ward Cleaver.

THEIR WEDDING, 1976

MARGE
I knew that my store was the right place for the wedding, all
these plants the perfect metaphor for growth and nurturance.
Lyn, let's get some photos over here by the carrot cake. And
where's your mother?—she should
be in this. I thought she was coming from Colorado.

LYN
Mom couldn't make it. She's getting *married*
herself. Isn't that fantastic? A masseur she met at Club Med.
Can you believe it?

EDIE
Hey, but Janet's here, so we'll get a video document of the whole
thing and send it to her.

MARGE
Edie, did you bring the contract?

Lyn, I told Edie to bring a contract like the one she has with Pam;
I want you and Bob to sign it. They've thought of everything.

Okay now,
over here by the cake.

FROM LYN'S JOURNAL

Was there ever a more wonderful wedding? Marge said we made
her believe in romance again.
Edie said we looked like organic Ken and Barbie
dolls. But whatever possessed us to
go on this transformational wilderness backpacking retreat?
It was a package deal—promising
higher consciousness and body awareness through mountain
climbing and transcendental trout fishing. Money back
guaranteed; the brochure said we would find ourselves.
Not only did we *not* find *ourselves,* we lost contact with the
rest of the group and spent our wedding night in the woods
sleeping on a bed of leaves that turned out to be poison ivy.
But we couldn't ask for our money back. Between our sexual
attraction for one another
and the poison ivy,
we had never *known* such body awareness.

AFTER THE HONEYMOON

L
Y
N

Whatever it is, Bob, it's the perfect wedding gift because it
comes from you. What is it?
A Geodesic Dome Home?
Kit? We have to build it ourselves?
But, Bob, you've been working on that isolation tank since before
we met
and it still leaks.

FROM LYN'S JOURNAL

The look on Bob's face when I made that remark about
his Samadhi tank is still with me.
It was the first squelching thing I've ever said to him.

AT THE RAPE CRISIS CENTER

L
Y
N

Hey, Edie, did Marge tell you about the great new P.R. job I have
with this big new clothing chain?

Well, okay, look, I mean . . . the job itself isn't all that great
but the person I'll be working under has a great
job, so there's lots of growth potential . . .

for *him* and then for *me,* I'm sure.

Telephone rings

Rape Crisis Hot Line.

Oh, no.
Oh, God. I can't believe it.
We'll be there in just a few minutes.

Redialing

Pam, meet us at Cedars.
The emergency room.
It's Marge.

A FEW WEEKS LATER

L
Y
N

Bob, honey, Marge called and wanted to come over.
She sounded so down. Daniel's left her; I said yes. I told her we
were finishing up the house and could use her touch and to
bring a plant or two.
This area really needs something, but no matter what I do, it still
looks like the living room of a flying saucer . . .
and have you noticed when you talk with your head tilted *up*,
there's an echo . . . echo . . . echo . . .
Maybe the ceiling wasn't meant to be this high, Bob . . . Bob . . .
Bob. I bet we added the garage pieces to the ceiling by mistake.
Now all we have left for the garage are these pieces
that are supposed to be
our closet.

Oh, well, since it's new, we'll have to give the Honda Civic our
closet space. I like their politics,
but we never should have bought a home advertised in
Mother Jones.

If we can't find the Dome Owner's Manual, we'll
just have to write for another.
Oh, there's Marge. I'll let her in. Honey, you
keep working on the tank.

M
A
R
G
E

For Christ's sake,
you don't need plants, you need Yosemite Park.
Hi. Bob, make me a drink, and make it a stiff one.
C'mon, you two, don't give me that look.
I've discovered a great medical cure for sobriety—
alcoholism!

But you don't have to pack me off to
Raleigh Hills treatment center quite yet. Hey, Bob, how's the
isolation tank?
You think it would help me? Hell, my whole life feels like one big
isolation tank. Okay, please, don't go to any trouble, you two;
I'll pour my own drink.

LYN

Marge, it's so ironic. I mean, that a woman as
nurturant as you could be so
self-destructive.

MARGE

I'll tell *you* what's ironic . . .
The rapist made off with my Mark Cross rape whistle.

BOB

I'm glad to see you looking so good.

LYN

The bruises are all gone.

MARGE

Yeah, the bruises *are* all gone.
Come on, let's unload the van.
Plants are gonna thrive here. They're gonna
think they died and went to heaven.

I've got japonicas, ficus, wonderful palms. Don't worry about the
tank, we'll cover it with ivy.

LYN

Thank heaven you're helping. My idea of what to do with a
room stops at throw pillows.

MARGE

All this room needs is a few decorative touches.
Like some right angles.
You two go on. I'm just gonna freshen my drink.

FROM LYN'S JOURNAL

> Marge is drinking more and more. Edie thinks she's doing
> coke a lot and drinks to take the edge off. Whatever
> it is, I'm worried.

IN THE DOME HOME

**L
Y
N**

Oh, Bob, I'm so excited. I'm getting a bigger office—no
partitions, real walls and a *door*. I think Sindell is
impressed. Oh, he still thinks I'm not a good
team player, that I do things my own way, but he's less
threatened by that now,
I think. But listen, let's not talk about my promotion when Edie
and Pam get here. Edie's newspaper's been bought out by Rupert
Murdoch. Pam said she's just heartsick.
There's the bell, at least that works. Try to be nice to Edie. I don't
know what it is with you two.

Edie, you know we're both so proud of you for quitting
your job. It was the only thing to do.

**E
D
I
E**

Quit, shit! I didn't get to quit. They *fired* my radical ass before I
could get the satisfaction.
Now I'm back working on my book,
"What's Left of the Left."
It's gonna be a slim volume, y'all.

Hey, did you hear, Pam's pioneer work in teaching men
to cry at her sensitivity seminars earned
her a paragraph in *Psychology Today*? I brought y'all a copy.
Bob, does this tank still leak, 'cause listen, now
it squeaks, too.
Lyn, you know, you should sign up Bob for Pam's next seminar,
"Anima, Animus, Animosity."
I got to commend you, Bob: Your solar thing you're into is
admirable, but this catalogue here, "Karma-Krafts."

Some of this stuff you're selling is New Age
chotchkes. I mean, there's some worthwhile stuff
here. These Bio-Bottom diapers—that sounds
okay. But most of this stuff is just New Age kitsch,
now admit it.
Look at this—aura goggles.
Here's some pyramid salt and pepper shakers.
"Key to the Universe" key chains. Oh, and these patchouli-
scented candles—guess that covers Indian philosophy.

Bumper stickers:
"If you think you are on the path, you are lost;
this is the Hollywood Freeway." Here's one I think I'll order:
"Honk! Honk! Honk! is not a mantra."

Bob, what yellow brick path are *you* on? Trying to mix
consumerism with higher consciousness,
you're liable to have a *big* karmic debt to pay. Hell, Bob, I recall
how you used to say
how we all had to look at success in a new way
or we'd never be truly successful. I used to dig you talkin' like
that 'cause it felt like you meant it.
I thought you were one of a handful of people left who cared
about not selling out. Remember all that shit about
"only wanting to do well if you could do good"?

BOB

You'll be interested to know I'm not doing
either. Now, isn't there a Flo Kennedy lecture or something you
have to rush off to?

LYN

Bob, please stop yelling. Pam, you're the shrink. What's with
these two?

EDIE

Aw, it's my fault. You know me. Pam says I get on my high horse
and stomp anything in sight. I'm sorry. Look, I've got Jiminy
Cricket damage.

PAM

She's too self-righteous for her own good, but we're
working on it.

FROM LYN'S JOURNAL

I feel bad that I didn't defend Bob when Edie picked on
him. I know Edie was hurting about her job, still I
should have tried to stop her.
She says herself she only lights into people she really cares for.
It's okay that she wants us to be more than we are; I want that,
too. But sometimes it's like she wants us to be more than we
can be. I don't really try to earn her approval anymore, but her
disapproval still bothers me.

A FEW MONTHS LATER, ON THE PHONE

L   Marge?
Y   Guess what?
N   I'm pregnant!
We're thrilled!
Even though we had planned to wait.

Bob's been singing "Having My Baby" all day.
I told him, "Keep singing that and I *will* throw up.
Again."

No, I haven't told the office, it might affect my job. This
morning I threw up at a board meeting. I was sure the cat was
out of the bag, but no one seemed to think anything about it;
apparently it's quite common for people to throw up
at board meetings.

What! How great! You helped? How?

Bob, Pam and Edie are having a baby, too!
Artificial insemination. Marge says it was easy.
They used a turkey baster, and now they're just letting nature
take its course.

FROM LYN'S JOURNAL

> Bob and I are so happy. Pam gave us a Piaget
> book we're reading to each other.
> Bob is being so sweet to me. He's going to be such a good father.
> And I'm going to be such a good mother.

SEVEN MONTHS LATER

L
Y
N

Twin boys! Honey, it must have been the water bed.

The doctor says they may both be hyperactive, but how bad could
these two little angels . . . be . . . Oh, you little tadpole!
Bob, quick—take one of them!
Honey, we have our hands full!
We can do it. We'll get superorganized; *this* time we'll
split the chores right down the middle.
We can have it all. We *already* have it all.
We just got it all at once, that's all.

ONE MORNING AT BREAKFAST

L
Y
N

Sweetheart, be honest—do you think I'm a good
mother? I mean, do *you* find it hard sometimes to tell the
twins apart?
Hildy says that I mix them up; of course, it's her word against
mine. We're not going to push them, but I want them to
have *all* the things we never had. Pam and Edie are already
giving Ivan violin lessons
and they're signing him up for a Tiny Tot
Transformation Seminar.

It's expensive, but let's sign up the twins.
Listen, I've got to run. Hildy will be here any minute.
Don't worry, I'm getting an assistant.
I've *asked* Sindell. Take some of the work load off.

Oh, no! Look at this—we bought the same bag again.

A MONTH LATER, AT THE OFFICE

L
Y
N

But, Bob, how could you forget that you have the twins tonight?
But you finished your sensitivity training last week. Why
would you sign up for an advanced class?
Honey, I don't think I can take you being any more *sensitive*.

Oh, I'm sorry. Listen, you're not tearing up, are you?
Look, I need this assertiveness training, Bob. I've got to
confront Sindell about that raise, and I've got to confront my
assistant, Tom.
He made a pass at me.
In front of everyone.
I think he really meant it as a put-down—
like some kind of perverse
power play. What do you think I should do? Confront him?
Let it slide? Or what?

What do you mean, "However I handle it is the way I should
handle it"?

FROM LYN'S JOURNAL

I worry sometimes,
maybe Bob has gotten too much in touch with
his feminine side. Last night, I'm pretty sure,
he faked an orgasm.

Marge picked the boys up at the office today, and when she
brought them back they were wearing little Indian cotton
drawstring pants, little baby Birkenstock sandals, their
T-shirts said "Small Is Beautiful." She must've had them made.
They looked just like Bob
did when we first met. She's so crazy about the twins, but
I worry when she has them; what if she should drink
too much?
Sometimes when the twins are sleeping I look down at them and
I feel this rush of tenderness and I am amazed at the love I
feel.

And *then* they wake up!

AT THE OFFICE, ON COFFEE BREAK

L   You don't know what it's like!
Y   Hyperactive twins!
N   When they turned three, my doctor prescribed Ritalin—
I wouldn't dream of giving drugs to my children,
but it does help when I take it myself.
I can't keep up with them.
At some point, they looked at one another,
realized there were two of them
and only *one* of me. Sometimes it gets so bad, I brew up some
Sleepytime herb tea, pour it over ice, serve it in Spiderman
glasses and
tell them it's a new-flavor
Kool-Aid.

I feel so guilty as I watch their little heads nod out.

Remember that rainy day last month I stayed home from the
office, sick?
They were unusually hyper. That day, I was desperate.
I said, "Do you want Mommy to teach you a new game?"

And I actually dragged them out to my car in the pouring rain,
put them in the backseat and told them,

"Stay there and play car wash."

Everyone around the coffee machine breaks up.

And Hildy is no help.
She lets them get away with murder.

I came home one day to find her stretched out on the floor,
motionless. I feared the worst. Suddenly, they leaped out,
jumped on Hildy, marked her earlobe with a Magic Marker.
Turns out they were playing *Wild Kingdom*,
Hildy was an elephant dying of thirst; she had to be tagged
and moved to a waterhole.

FROM LYN'S JOURNAL

When I'm telling people about the twins, it suddenly
hits me how adorable they are. But when I'm actually
dealing with them, sometimes I go into such overwhelm.
I feel jittery and tired at the same time.
I wanted to be this wonderfully understanding mother—always
loving, patient.
Maybe if I cut out coffee—drink decaf and maybe some
B-complex.

I don't want Bob and the twins to look back and
remember me this way.

Funny,
I went into public relations because I have a way with people.
Just not the people I'm closest to.

My therapist told me this journal writing sometimes
relieves depression.

But it's the things that come up when I'm writing in my journal
that seem to depress me.
This morning I went to kiss the twins
goodbye, they saw Hildy coming in, left me
and ran to kiss her hello.

AT THE OFFICE, ON THE PHONE

L
Y
N

Marge, I'm so sorry to cancel lunch again.
It's been a terrible day.
I just had to fire Chrissy. Oh, it's been building up
ever since I hired her. Can you use someone
with no skills?

She gets everything confused. She got my
lunch date with an important client mixed
up with where the twins were to go for a
birthday party.

So I arrive and see my client waiting for me
outside Chuck E. Pizza-Time Theatre.

No, this weekend is out.
Sindell really wants me to do this
seminar/conference thing. I'm embarrassed to tell you:
"Woman on the Way Up." I felt insulted at first,
but it's just his way of telling me he wants me to be a corporate
clone. I know he's got bigger and better things in mind.
I can't let up now. I feel like I'm being watched every second to
see if I make
the right moves.

Oh, I know the twins would love to go,
but they've got a busier weekend than mine.

No, not tonight.
Tonight I've got Bob. Seems like we never
see each other lately unless we sign up for the same seminar.

This morning at breakfast,
I was going over my calendar.

He asked me if I was going to pencil him in
for sex
on the weekend.
How is it being back with Daniel? Is it working out?

Oh.
I'm sorry, but maybe it's for the best.

I mean, I know you say you love him,
but you haven't been happy with him.
Can't you just let him go this time without all the pain?
Oh, there's my phone. Sindell, I bet. I have to go.
Call you later. Yes, yes, I *promise.*

IN THE DOME HOME

L
Y
N

Bob, I'm home! Honey, I'm sorry to be late.
The last lecture just went on and on. I'll try to get home early
tomorrow; I'll fix something special for dinner. Right now, I just
want to get these shoes off
and fix a drink. I don't know how I functioned before this
seminar, Bob.
I learned "desktop gardening," "office isometrics" and "power
dressing," a new fashion trend where you
wear something around the neck that looks
sort of like a scarf
and sort of like a tie
and sort of like a ruffle
and doesn't threaten anyone,
because you don't look good in it.
Look! I'm proof. Does this look like a woman on the way up?
Bob, what's wrong?

Where are you going? Your aikido class? I didn't even know you
were taking aikido.
When did you start taking aikido?

You're not mad, are you?

LATER THAT NIGHT, ON THE PHONE

L
Y
N

Edie, Marge called the other day.
I can't stop worrying about her. She wanted
to take the twins someplace again. I had
to say no. Bob says he doesn't even want the twins
to be around her anymore at all. I think she knows we're cutting
her off from them,
but what can we do? She adores them, and they adore her,
but the last time I picked them up, I found her
on the floor. I thought they were playing *Wild Kingdom* again,
but turns out she was drunk and had fallen.
We think now she's taking pills
along with everything else.

Did you know Daniel split again? He just never
got over the rape. I don't think she has, either.
And I don't know that she'll ever get over Daniel.
Could you go by tonight, see if she's okay?
Bob's just walked out in a huff, so I've got the kids, or I'd go.

Just a minute.
Come on, boys! Supper's almost ready. Settle
down. You know our agreement—if you're going to fight,
use your Bataca encounter bats.

Edie, is that little Ivan I hear playing the
violin? Amazing! I'd swear it was Isaac Stern.
I'll get him a set of Bataca bats. Bob sells them.
We better
start protecting those genius hands.
I tell you, the twins are *much* less aggressive.

Listen, if you know of someone, I need a housekeeper. I
can't afford it, but Hildy won't lift a finger to help around the
house, except for the twins. Somehow, a cluttered dome home
looks worse
than a cluttered tract house; all the clutter seems to
circle back on itself. Last week, in desperation, I
just picked up all the junk, tossed it into the
Samadhi tank, and forgot about it. That is, until
Bob started testing it, and filled the tank with water. Oh, God,
Edie, it began to overflow and out came all the stuff I'd
forgotten about.
And I'm not proud of this,
but, well, I let Bob think
the twins had done it.

If I'd known this is what it would be like to
have it all,
I might have been willing to settle
for less.

IN THE DOME HOME

L
Y
N

Please don't complain about the cleaning not being back;
I can't take one more complaint! I'll tell you why the cleaning's
not back.
I forgot to take it, okay? Bob, you expect too much
of me. It's one thing to be a modern housewife,
career woman, mother. I could handle being
modern. Modern is popping a frozen dinner into
the microwave, but modern isn't good enough for
you. No, I have to be organic,
holistic,
learn millet recipes,
grow wheat grass, make *beet* juice,
wait around for sourdough to rise. Well, it just so happens the
last sourdough we had wasn't sourdough—
it was Play-Doh.

Oh, the twins have a highly developed sense of humor, and *we*
didn't even notice the *difference,* Bob. So much for
conscious cooking.

And the Ecology Pageant at school. Robert wants to go as
a nuclear reactor,
McCord wants to go as the hundredth monkey.
You think I can
buy costumes like that at K Mart? No, I have
to *make* them. Edie and Pam don't sew, of course, so I told
them I'd make Ivan a Solar Energy costume—
only now he doesn't want to go as that.
He wants to go as an endangered species!

And wok cooking! You said it was fast! It *is*
fast. *What takes time*
is having to go to
Chinatown
for all those Chinese vegetables!
I'm so sick of your disappointment in me; I'm disappointed too.
I see now you're not so damn Zen, after all; you're passive-
aggressive. Somehow, we both mistook that for
spirituality.

And your acting like you've transcended your
ego is the biggest ego trip of all!

FROM LYN'S JOURNAL

I don't think I've ever seen Bob so angry.
He threw things up to me:
All the times I'd been late.
All the weekends I'd been gone.
He threw things up to me I'd totally forgotten about.
He brought up that time I let the clothes pile up for so long,
by the time I got around to it, the twins had outgrown the
ironing.

It's clear what Bob and I both need:
a *wife*!

TWO PHONE CALLS

L
Y
N

I had no idea they'd taken the bats to school with
them. Believe me, it will *not* happen again.

Look, just give me a *list* of the damage and I will
pay for it.

I'm sorry, I'm raising two Darth Vaders.

The other call

L
Y
N

   Oh, Bob, something terrible.
   Marge is dead!
   She's hanged herself.
   They found her hanging from a macramé planter.
   What do you mean, *how*?
   I guess she took the plant *out* and put her *head* in!
   Oh, Bob, if only I hadn't put off seeing her; I shouldn't have cut
   her off from the twins.

FROM LYN'S JOURNAL, 1982

I knew she was in pain. How could I have thought I was getting
through to her when all I did was nag and criticize, and when
that didn't work, I just withdrew. Bob said I did all I could to help
her, but I have to face the fact it's not true.

We had a memorial service at her store.
We cried and then we got stoned on her sinsemilla.
Then we laughed until we cried again.

Janet was there. I asked about Agnus. She told
me that she'd lost custody, that Agnus had been
living with her father and his new wife, but had
run away. The look on her face when she talked
about Agnus. I can't stop thinking about it—
all those missing children you hear so much about. To
think now Agnus is one of them.

I felt so grateful for Bob and the kids. From now on,
I will be *Mega*-Mom,
Wonder
Working
Woman,
Willing Wife.

> I will even be the Total Woman . . .
> at least for a night or two.
> I don't want us to lose
> what we have.

A FEW MONTHS LATER, AT THE OFFICE

L Oh, Edie, I can't go to the conference this weekend.
Y I've got to finish this campaign.
N

Office buzzer

> Hear that?
> Just a second.
>
> I told you to tell Sindell I will be there in
> a moment.

Back with Edie

> Look, I'll write a check right now. How should I make it out?
> Oh, I can't find my checkbook—oh, no wonder, I've got Bob's bag
> again . . .
> uh, look, I'll call you later.

Office buzzer buzzes again and again

> Tell Sindell I'll be right in.
>
> I really have to say to you I was sure you were
> thinking of me for that promotion. I mean, for you
> to hire someone from outside the company
> to do a job you *know* I can do because I have been
> *doing* it . . . *and* my own job . . .

But I'm really glad it's all out in the open.
You've been holding out this new position, making me try to
prove myself to you
over and over again by outperforming everybody else,
staying late, taking work home . . .

LATER THAT NIGHT

L   I wanted to take the scarf-ruffle-tie thing from
Y   around my neck
N   and *strangle* him.
    I had no choice but to quit.

It's been a *great* day, Bob . . . oh, by the way, here—
I took your bag again today, by mistake.

I tore up the letter, if that's what you're looking for.

How could I not have known you were involved with someone. I
can't believe it. How long?

Who is it? Some horny herbalist?
Is it that checkout girl at the Health-Mart?

All those nights you were gone . . . I should've known
you couldn't have that many
aikido classes each week.
Who is it?!

Your aikido instructor?

Oh, I can just imagine what she's like.
If she knows aikido,
she probably knows the *Kamasutra.*
You're probably having this great tantric sex thing.
Are you?

I'm sure she's *more evolved* than I am, isn't she? *More centered!* Isn't that their big thing, centeredness?

She probably has time to make good money *and* to meditate.

Don't *tell* me her tofu tastes like lasagna. She knows what
shape face she has and where she's going
and how to get there
neatly.

If only I'd been taking karate classes; I would love for these
hands to be *weapons!*

Feel free to interrupt me at any time.

FROM LYN'S JOURNAL

How could I not have known?
All those disagreements, irritations, misunderstandings,
expectations, disappointments, complaints—always
unresolved. Where did I think all this would lead?
I can forgive Bob;
it's harder to forgive myself. I could change my thinking
and decide to release it. I could change myself, but I can't
change the fact
that Bob really *is* involved.

AT THE DOCTOR'S

L   You're sure, Doctor?
Y   Premenstrual syndrome?
N   I mean, I'm getting divorced.
      My mother's getting divorced.
      I'm raising twin boys.
      I have a lot of job pressure—
      I've got to find one.
      The ERA didn't pass,
      not long ago I lost a very dear friend, and . . . and
      my husband is involved . . .
      not just involved, but in love, I'm afraid . . . with this
      woman . . .
      who's quite a bit younger than I am.

      And you *think* it's my *period*
      and *not* my life?

THE OLD HANGOUT

The Jukebox: Tina Turner, "Let's Stay Together"

E
D
I
E

Promise me you won't cry at what I've got to tell you.
'Cause if *you* do, *I* will,
and you know what an ugly sight *that* is.
Pam and I are moving to New York. Ivan
got that violin scholarship, and Pam's got a good offer—new
magazine they're starting, *Today's Mind.*
They want Pam on the staff. And me? I got stuff cooking there;
Bella may run again.
We got Janet's loft while she's away on some worldwide tour
with that damn art piece of hers.
Now she calls it "A Get-Well Card to the Avant-Garde."
I hear she does that part under the veil herself. Yeah, Ivan's
gonna play a solo with that Suzuki group of kids at Carnegie
Hall. Can you believe that turkey-baster kid is a prodigy? I
knew we had something special when he was born on
Thanksgiving.
He cries about leaving the twins; they've been his good
buddies. Ah, you know how those bullies at school gang up on
him, playing the violin the way he does.
Got one green eye, one blue.
Got two mommies and no daddy.
Pam and I should never have gone to that
PTA meeting together.
But anybody picked on him, those twins were like two little
Charlie Bronsons with Bataca bats.
So what about you?
You're back in the work farce, huh?

L
Y
N

Import/export. I'm a partner, Edie.
They put in all the money
and I put in all my time.

We import ethnic clothing, mostly from South
America. And no, don't say it; I don't think we're exploiting
cheap labor, so much as I think we're giving work to people
who would be out of work . . .
if *we* weren't exploiting cheap labor.
Oh, Edie, I know what you're thinking, but
it's hard to be politically conscious and upwardly mobile
at the same time.

How naive. To think there was a time when we actually thought
we were going to change the system. And all the time . . .

.

FROM LYN'S JOURNAL, AUGUST 1984

Bob and I told the twins
that since we'd be seeing them at different times,
they'd have twice as much "quality time." But
they didn't buy it.
All I can think of is all
the mistakes I've made
and is this divorce going to be
another one.

I called Edie tonight during the nomination.
We stayed on the phone together.

When we heard "Ladies and gentlemen of the
convention, my name is
Geraldine Ferraro,"
we cried. Earlier, when the newscaster
on ABC had said,
"She's kept her maiden name,
not for any feminist reason,
but because she feels she owes
her mother so much,"
we laughed.

I thought to myself: There was a time when Edie
wouldn't have laughed at that.
It was so good to hear her voice.
I must remember to send Ivan a telegram
about his concert at Carnegie Hall.

WITH BOB AT THE LAWYER'S

L
Y
N

I took the boys to see Santa Claus. When Santa Claus asked
Robert what he wanted for Christmas, Robert said,
"A nuclear freeze."
And then McCord yanked Santa's beard off and said,
"What animal got killed for this?"
I knew you'd be proud.

I mean, for a kid that age to have the spirit to confront Santa
Claus on what he thought was a *moral* issue . . . Well . . .

Maybe we did *some* things right, after all.

BACK AT THE GARAGE SALE

L
Y
N

Yes, there *is* something odd-looking about a garage sale outside a dome home. Especially when it's in your closet.

Yes, everything goes, even the house. Look, over there we still have the boxes that it *came* in.

This? This is a Samadhi flotation tank. It leaks. But, look, it makes a wonderful . . . storage bin. It's a little hard to open now, because of all that ivy growing over the door.
Yes, everything inside goes.
Oh, except this—
this old autographed copy of *Ms.* magazine . . .
and this T-shirt,
"Whales Save Us."
I'm keeping these.

T
R
U
D
Y

What a concert!
We've been having an electromagnetic
field day.
Pun intended.

Just listen . . . amazing . . . in my head, I can still hear
that violin concert.
What *is* it in our brains that lets us recall the music
after it's over? Why is it when we hear certain music
we get a lump in our throat? My space chums wonder how come
we don't get the lump in our ear. They're impressed with
our ability to get lumps in the throat. Apparently, we're
unique in that respect. They wanted to know if it felt
anything like goose bumps. I said, "You never felt goose bumps,
either?" They said, "No." They asked me to explain goose bumps—
do they come from the heart?
Do they come from the soul? Do they come from the brain?
Or do they come from
geese?
This set us waxing philosophic! All this searching. All these
trances, all this data, and all we *really* know is
how *little* we know about what it *all* means. Plus, there's the
added question of what it *means* to *know* something.
Scientists say for every deep truth discovered, the opposite is also
true. So when we get the feeling we're going around in circles—
no wonder, we *are!*

They said, "Trudy, we see now, intelligence is just the tip
of the iceberg. The more you know,
the less knowing the *meaning* of things means.
So *forget* the meaning of life."
I didn't tell them, of course,
I had.
See, it's not so much *what* we know,
but *how* we know, and what
it is about us that *needs* to know.

The intriguing part: Of all the things we've learned, we still
haven't learned
where did this desire to *want* to know *come from*?
Oh, don't look at me. This is the way they *talk*.

We know a lot about the beginnings of life. Bio-genesis.
But so what? What's more impressive is that from bio-genesis
evolved life forms intelligent enough to think up a word like
"bio-genesis."

So no matter how much we know, there's more to knowing than
we could ever know.

Sir Isaac Newton . . . secretly admitted to some friends: He
understood how gravity *behaved*, but not how it *worked*!

The operative word here is what?
Apple!
Who said "Soup"?

We're thinking maybe the secrets about life we don't understand
are the "cosmic carrots" in front of our noses that keep us going.
So maybe we should stop trying to figure out the *meaning* of
life and sit back and enjoy

the *mystery* of life.
The operative word
here is what?
Mystery!
Not meaning.

This should be comforting, especially to those who think life is
meaningless. It just might *be,* which could explain
why we have so many
meaningless things in our lives.

And yet, if life is *meaningless*—
this is the greatest *mystery* of all!

Even this feeling we get in the pit of our stomach
when we contemplate how meaningless it all seems
is part of the mystery.

And the more meaningless,
then the greater the mystery.

But if all this is meaningless, then why the hell bring up
the subject? If *life* is meaningless, this *discussion* is even
more so.

This is so *typical* of what I *do.*
I feel like a mammalian-brained lunkhead.
We thought about all this, but not for long,
because no matter how expanded your mind gets,
your span of concentration remains
as short as ever.

Next, they insisted I take them somewhere
so they could get goose bumps. They were dying to see
what it was like.

I decided maybe we should take in a play.
I got goose bumps once that way.
So we headed back toward Shubert Alley.

On the way to the play, we stopped to look at the stars.
And as usual,
I felt in awe.
And then I felt even deeper in awe at this capacity we have to
be
in awe about something.

Then I became even more awestruck
at the thought that I was,
in some small way,
a part of that
which I was in awe about.

And this feeling went on
and on
and on. . . .
My space chums got a word for it:
"awe infinitum."

Because at the point you can comprehend how
incomprehensible it all is,
You're about as smart as you need to be.

Suddenly I burst into song:
"Awe,
sweet mystery of life,
at last I've found thee."

And I felt so good inside
and my heart felt so full,

I decided I would set time aside each day to do
awe-robics.

Because at the moment you are most in awe of all there is
about life that you don't understand,
you are closer to understanding it all
than at any other time.

KATE   Oh, Lonnie, you look drenched, but doesn't the rain feel good?
I've had the most extraordinary evening.
Waiter, two brandies.
Since I've seen you, so much has happened
I feel like a new person.

No, it's not my new fingertip.

Good, though, isn't it?

No, this evening, first this little boy played the violin—
absolute genius!

Before I forget, here's that article I had Xeroxed for you—all
about boredom, remember?

Oh, no, no, no, no. Sorry, that's not it. That's my suicide note.

Well, not *my* suicide note . . .
It's one I've been keeping because,
well, I found it,
and I haven't been able to throw it away, because . . .
well, I don't know exactly, it's the strangest effect. . . .
Where shall I start?

When I was in L.A. I found this suicide note in the
street where my exercise class is. I don't know why I
picked it up. You know, it's more my nature to step *over*
things.

But something compelled me. . . .

I thought
it could be a sign.
Lately, I seem to look for signs; the closer I get to
menopause, the more metaphysical I'm becoming.

I had no idea who it belonged to. *Anyone* living in *that*
neighborhood had *reason* to want to end it all. I couldn't
bring myself to throw it away. There should be a
service one could use in cases like this, but there isn't.

I was saddened by what she said in the note—
but I felt even worse when I realized that losing the
note could only *add* to her feelings of low self-esteem.
Further evidence she could never do
anything right. I should
imagine there's only one thing more depressing than writing a
suicide note,
and that's *losing* the one you've just written.

For a while, I kept it in my wallet. And then I grew concerned.
Well, supposing I got hit by a car, or, in that neighborhood, a
beer bottle, I go unconscious, the paramedics come, they
discover the note, they think it's mine and they give it to
Freddie.

Well, it would seem very strange that I just happened to be
carrying someone else's suicide note.

So I started keeping it at home.
In one of those fireproof boxes with my important papers. Then
the thought, again, what if something happened?

The note would be discovered and be given great importance because it was with my important papers.

So I began moving it around the house.
Lonnie, I am becoming so forgetful. I was so afraid I would misplace it. So I wrote myself a note telling me where I'd put it.

Now I had the suicide note *and* the note telling me *where* the suicide note was hidden.
So I have decided it is best kept in my purse. But don't worry—I've written a note explaining the whole business.

Go ahead and say it: I am *possessed.* What is it about this phantom person that is so compelling?
She seemed so fragile and yet courageous, too. Ironically, there is in this suicide note more feeling, more forgiveness, more capacity for life . . .
Whatever this person is, or was, she was *not* jaded. She was not bored. Her only real complaint was something she called "false hopes."
If she ever *did* commit suicide, it would be out of feeling too much—not too little.

There's hardly a trace of bitterness or petty *anything.* That's really something, don't you think?
I mean, in writing a suicide note, the *real* person must come out.

There was nothing dramatic—
no big tragedy,
no terminal illness—
it seems, just,
a lifetime of being . . .

dismissed . . . by everyone, apparently . . .
except me.

Lonnie, this experience has had such an effect on me. Made me
aware of just how closed off I've been to people's suffering,
even my own.

This evening, after the concert, I saw these two prostitutes on
the corner . . . talking with this street crazy, this bag lady.
And I actually stopped to watch them. Even though it had begun
to rain.

And I remembered something I think it was Kafka wrote about
having been filled with a sense of endless astonishment at
simply seeing a group of people cheerfully assembled.

I saw this young man go up, obviously from out of town, and he
asked them, "How do I get to Carnegie Hall?" And the bag lady
said, "Practice!" And we caught each other's eyes—the
prostitutes, the bag lady, the young man and I.
We all burst out laughing.

There we were, laughing together, in the pouring rain, and then
the bag lady did the dearest thing—
she offered me her umbrella hat.

She said that I needed it more than she did, because one side
of my hair was beginning to
shrink.

And, Lonnie, I did the strangest thing.

I took it!

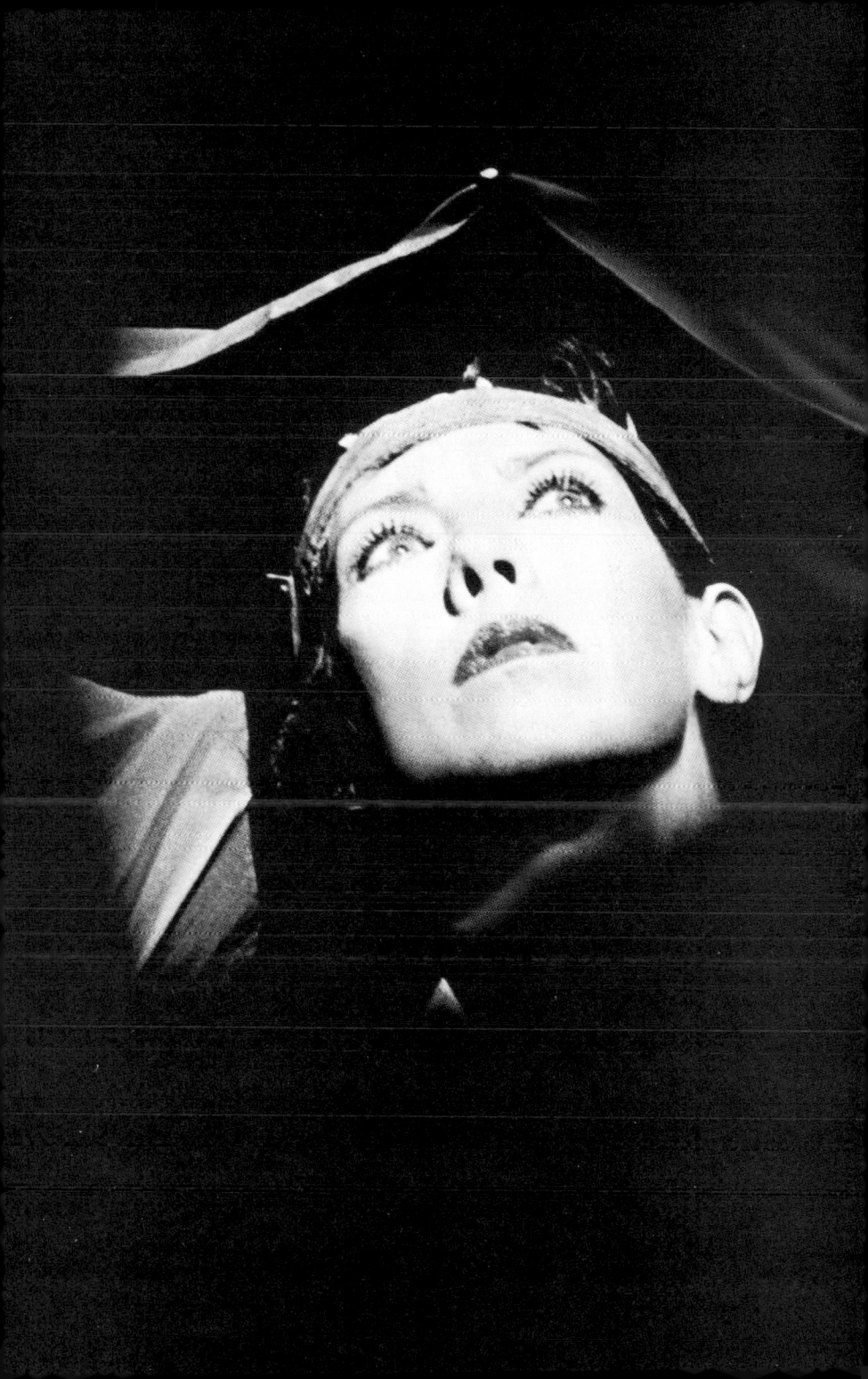

Hey, what's this?

"Dear Trudy, thanks for making our stay here so jam-packed and
fun-filled. Sorry to abort our mission—it is not over,
just temporarily scrapped.

We have orders to go to a higher bio-vibrational plane.

Just wanted you to know, the neurochemical imprints of our
cardiocortical experiences here on earth will remain with us
always, but what we take with us into space that we cherish the
most is the 'goose bump' experience."

Did I tell you what happened at the play? We were at the back
of the theater, standing there in the dark,
all of a sudden I feel one of 'em tug my sleeve,
whispers, "Trudy, look." I said, "Yeah, goose bumps. You
definitely
got goose bumps. You really like the play that much?" They said
it wasn't the play
gave 'em goose bumps,
it was the audience.

I forgot to tell 'em to watch the play; they'd been watching
the *audience*!

Yeah, to see a group of strangers sitting together in the dark,
laughing and crying about the same things . . . that just knocked
'em out.
They said, "Trudy,
the play was soup . . .
the audience . . .
art."

So they're taking goose bumps
home with 'em.
Goose bumps!
Quite a souvenir.

I like to think of them out there
in the dark, watching us.
Sometimes we'll do something and they'll laugh.
Sometimes we'll do something and they'll cry.
And maybe one day we'll do something so magnificent,
everyone in the universe will get
goose bumps.

AFTERWORD

BY MARILYN FRENCH

LAST FALL, SOMETHING NEW HAPPENED IN THE CULTURAL LIFE OF America, something that should hearten and encourage every person who believes this nation needs humane redirection: a show opened on Broadway starring Lily Tomlin, written by Jane Wagner, and called *The Search for Signs of Intelligent Life in the Universe.* Whoa! you say. Sure we know Lily Tomlin is great, but how can a Broadway show matter that much? (Even though there are plans to take the show on a worldwide tour later this year, and to tape it as a special for cable television and the home video market.)

Lily Tomlin made her first reputation on television, the most far-reaching of all cultural media. Millions of people are familiar with the characters she created on the comedy series *Laugh-In* and followed her and her longtime collaborator Jane Wagner as they expanded Tomlin's comic repertory in Emmy Award–winning television specials and an earlier Broadway show, *Appearing Nitely,* which won a Tony.

The Search for Signs of Intelligent Life in the Universe focuses on female—one might well say *human*—experience of society. It looks at a world that is pervaded by the drive to power, but it is also a hilarious running critique of our society, so accurate and humane that *New York Times* critic Frank Rich called it "the most genuinely subversive comedy to be produced on Broadway in years." One man's subversive is another's (woman or man) truth: what is most extraordinary about the Tomlin/Wagner show is the degree of truth about American society that it dares to present on a public stage to an audience educated by the artificial sunshine and artificial violence of most television and movies—action without reverberations, people without character, like Marisol cut-out figures.

The major narrator of the performance is Trudy, a bag lady who has been "certified" mad, but whose madness is really a perception of society from the underside, the kind of seeing that Socrates called "a divine release of the soul from the yoke of custom and convention." Trudy is wise, acute, funny. Her voice and face appear, then vanish as other characters appear— Chrissy, a young woman who lacks direction and spends hours in a health club (sometimes she has a male counterpart); Kate, a wealthy woman suffering from "affluenza" ("a bored species cannot survive"); Agnus Angst, an unhappy punk adolescent who tries to use Gordon Liddy's book *Will* as a guide to life; and an entire community of friends who have been together throughout the feminist movement (dated by the script from the Women's Strike for Equality) and who are unsure of what to do now. Tomlin moves from one role to another swiftly, unerringly, and brilliantly characterizes each of these figures. We always know who is speaking, yet she does not depend on facile mannerisms, props or costumes to distinguish them. She *moves into* them, she becomes her characters from the inside as only a great actress can.

The point of view of the show is actually from the lowest social stratum in American society. This is intentional. Tomlin and Wagner both came from rural Southern families, although Tomlin was raised in Detroit, in a blue-collar neighborhood, among people who, she feels, did not recognize the degree to which their suffering was caused by a system rather than by each other, that "the system" was only a system, and not the very law of nature. But compassion is handled lightly in *The Search for Signs of Intelligent Life in the Universe*—Jane Wagner's script is unsentimental. Not until the end of the show do Kate and Trudy—who represent the poles of female wealth and poverty— encounter each other, and when they do, the meeting is comic as well as significant.

Nor does Wagner's script deal out blame for the social problems it addresses. Instead it focuses on our anxiety and on our dangerous tendency to harden ourselves. Agnus Angst comments, "Wow, breathing is a bio-hazard. If we don't take in air every few minutes, we die, but the air we are taking in is killing us. I rush to my Behavioral Modification Center, hoping they can help me cut down on my habit of *breathing.*" She repeats an overheard conversation: "Do you want to stop *drinking?*" "No. . . . " "Do you want to stop *overeating?*" "No. I want to stop caring that I eat, drink and smoke too much!" She offers an idea for a new marketing business venture for a new religion: behavior modification for people who want to stop caring about anything. She tries to resuscitate a goldfish that dies of living in drinking water; she recites, "I want my skin to thicken/so if I am panic-stricken/when post-nuke day gets here/I won't even feel the fear/as I watch me and the world disappear."

Meeting Tomlin and Wagner one October afternoon just after the show opened on Broadway, I was struck by the apparent fact that they do not have a prepared "rap," a public facade to protect themselves against interviewers. They both seem beautifully open. Lily wanders when she speaks, and is not comfortable with generalizations or abstractions; she talks in a calm quiet voice about people, scenes and actions that have been significant for her. She has an artist's acuity for the gesture or mannerism that characterizes a person beneath the level of speech. Jane focuses on words, speech, absurdities in attitudes, but she too prefers the concrete, the particular. Neither expresses herself righteously or in anger, although both allow themselves to perceive misery and consider what they can do to alleviate it. Lily describes a homeless young man who came up to her in Central Park on the day Yoko Ono was dedicating Strawberry Fields, came up to her among others, and hit her lightly on the arm, repeating over and over, "We could feed the whole fucking world today, man, today! Not next month or in ten years! Today!" Lily believes he is right.

Most of popular culture and what is designated "high art" emerges from a traditional masculinist perspective: certain attitudes toward women, nature, domination, male individualism and power are simply taken for granted. And a major criticism leveled at feminist art by masculinists (male or female) is that it tends to belabor its points rather than simply assume them. But feminist art *has* to belabor its points—has to inform its audience that everything that exists is interconnected, that dominance is factitious, that body and emotion are as important as mind, and that these three are more important than domination—because these ideas diverge from the mainstream. *The Search for Signs of Intelligent Life in the Universe* is the first work I know of that simply takes it as a given that a mass audience will accept feminist attitudes, that proceeds on the assumption these attitudes are shared and that therefore does not lecture, hector or even underline. As I was leaving Tomlin's dressing room, I remarked that this show was a breakthrough, that they could not have put it on Broadway ten years ago. Jane Wagner looked at me with surprise: "You think so? I don't know. I guess we're so involved with what we're doing that we don't think about how it will be received. Not that it doesn't matter to us . . . but maybe we aren't really on that wavelength."

Innocents abroad-way, I think, creating a show the theme of which is voiced by Trudy: "You'd think by now evolution could've at least evolved us to the place where we could change ourselves." Underlying the gentle laughter that is a Tomlin/ Wagner hallmark is the conviction that we have some power to alter the course of our world as well as our own lives. And that message is received by the audience. The atmosphere of the theater is intense, magnetized; the roar afterward conveys the feeling one had as one sat there, that people were starving for truth in art, and had finally been fed, and knew it.

Not to wonder. Trudy has a recurrent motif; she keeps trying to remind herself that there is a difference between art (as exemplified by Andy Warhol's silk-screened prints of Campbell's Soup cans) and the soup itself. "Art . . . Soup," she ruminates; "Soup . . . Art." She is confused because she sees through the mystifications of culture, and knows that art *is* soup—that is, it is nourishment. Art is not the intellectual pyrotechnics of a "superior" mind, nor the delicate expression of an exquisite, rarefied sensibility. Art is food. We need it.

The show concludes with Trudy musing about mysteries— among them the catharsis (Aristotle's word, not hers—although she does quote Socrates) that results from people who are "strangers, sitting together in the dark," watching truth enacted before them, "laughing and crying about the same things," together. Through art, especially in the theater, our small isolate lives, our quiet perceptions (never uttered, either for lack of words or for lack of an other to whom we can say such things), can be joined, can merge together in an ecstatic rush that alleviates our loneliness and helps to give direction, a moral perspective to our lives.

Art does this. Lily Tomlin and Jane Wagner do this. And they are doing it seven times a week on a public stage, playing to packed houses made up of us—all of us. Don't tell me feminism is dead! It's alive and well and living at the Plymouth Theater, Broadway, New York (and in San Diego, Los Angeles, Seattle, Portland, Houston, Lexington, Atlanta, Aspen and Boston all places where Tomlin performed and Wagner revised this show as a work in progress). It is living in the audience, made up of men as well as women, mostly young, but not all. When the show is over, and Lily Tomlin, no doubt exhausted, finally refuses to come out yet again, the audience keeps clapping, clapping, sending a message, telling her, telling each other, that they have that night received the gift of truth.

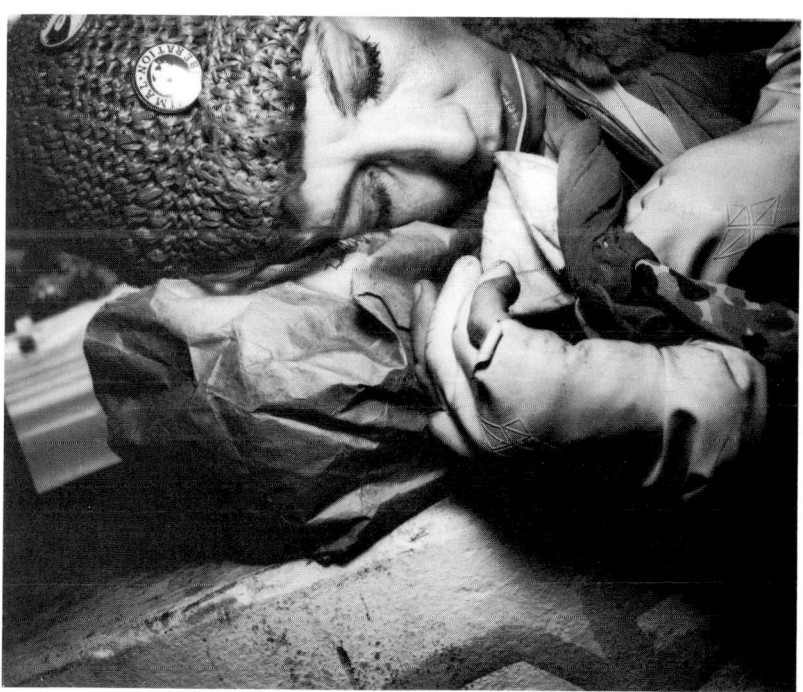

Special Photo Insert

THE FILM

with original set sketches
by Nando Scarfiotti

Street philosopher Trudy waits in her corner of reality to consult with aliens from hyperspace.

Chrissy at the Health Club perfects her body as she talks about the mess her life is in.

Kate at the Beauty Salon frets about her boring life and her bad haircut.

Kate at the Cocktail Lounge talks about a mysterious suicide note.

Agnus Angst performs her act at the Anti-Club.

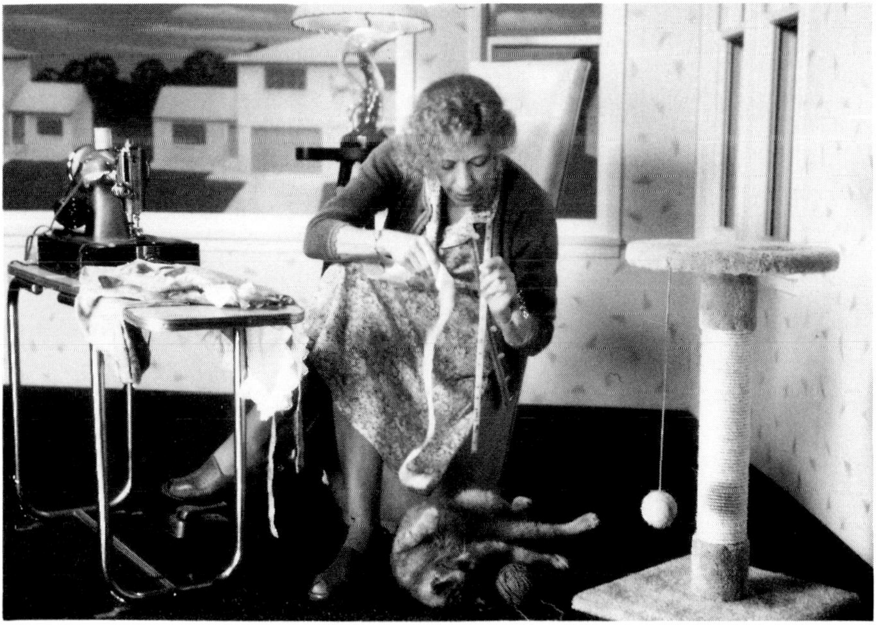

Lud and Marie relax at home.

Trudy orders a chocolate soda and a side of fried clams.

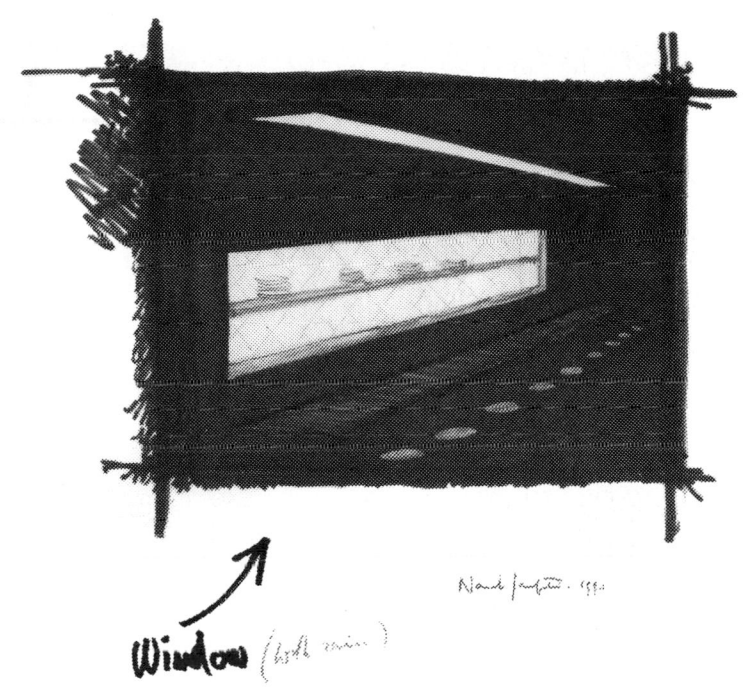

Window (with rain)

Trudy smells something good that Howard's cooking.

Brandy and Tina, two entrepreneurial hookers

1970 – WOMEN'S STRIKE FOR EQUALITY

1970 New York – Aug 26
EDIE & MARGE & I were there –
marching with 50,000!!!
others down 5ᵗʰ Ave.. The Senate
is holding "ERA" hearings for
the first time since 1956.
I know we are going to
  CHANGE IT ALL !!!

Trudy time-traveling

Trudy at home